WALKING THROUGH SHADOWS

A few stamps from my pilgrims' credential.

WALKING THROUGH SHADOWS

El Camino de Santiago de Compostela

Carl Sesto

Sabbatical Press 2011

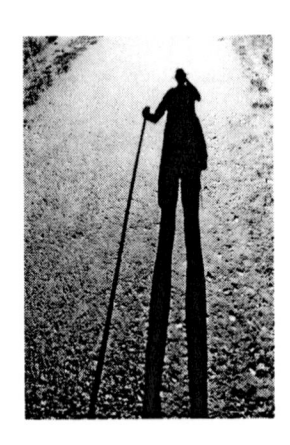

While any pilgrimage begins where you are,

the walking part of my pilgrimage

began in France in a small village

called St. Jean Pied-de-Port

on June 18, 1997 and

ended 800 kilometers away

in Spain in Santiago de Compostela

on July 24, 1997.

PROLOGUE

"Not quite a full shilling," Win says as we trudge along el Camino de Santiago de Compostela. She is referring to her assessment of the general condition of pilgrims we've met. Win is a Netherlander who I encounter every now and then and sometimes walk with. Today we are walking on a dirt cart path in mid-afternoon under a blazing Spanish sun. She has a handkerchief on her head as a makeshift hat. Although it is an unseasonably cool summer, the temperature being somewhere around 82 degrees, the sun is brutal and I check to see if I am actually wearing my dark sunglasses. I am, but every now and then it seems so bright I'm convinced I've forgotten to put them on. "Now that you mention it…" I respond, thinking about where I come up short of the shilling and why I decided to make the pilgrimage in the first place. I mentally run through the people we know in common and realize that Win may have boiled it all down to a phrase that accurately describes our pilgrims. "What about the Norwegian couple?" I ask, just as a way of testing the theory. A retired couple, the Norwegians seem, on the surface, to be completely unassailable in the shilling department. They have generously given me bandages and in the last village they jumped up from where they were sitting having coffee as I walked across the street just to greet me and ask how I was doing. "They have each other," Win says. Not a totally convincing counterargument, but I accept it in the blinding sun and quick pace we've set on our way to Villar de Mazarife, a small village about 25 km from León. About a week and a half later, Cas, a Dutchman, and I were having dinner in a restaurant in Santa Irene. We listed nine reasons pilgrims undertake the arduous journey—but that's later.

Magic forest encountered crossing the Pyrenees.

June 18, 1997

St. Jean-Pied-de-Port–B & B

I started my pilgrimage with a visit to Madame Debril in the picturesque French village of St. Jean Pied-de-Port. From my readings, it seemed this was a common place to begin, having the dual qualities of crossing a national boundary and walking over the Pyrenees Mountains with spectacular views. I felt I was as ready as I was ever going to be for my journey, my pilgrimage. For the previous month I had regularly practiced walking in the L.L. Bean hiking boots my daughter gave me for the trip. Two weeks before departure, I finally broke down and bought a backpack, sleeping bag, and other assorted hiking gear, most of which I didn't need, and practiced hiking around town fully equipped, or, as it turned out, over equipped. I didn't really believe in over preparation. My theory was that short of actually doing the pilgrimage twice, once in my hometown north of Boston, and then for real in Spain, there was no point in overdoing the practice sessions. For one thing, I didn't want to walk 800 km around town. I'm much too lazy for that and, in addition, it's boring to have to walk back to your starting point every time, essentially going in circles. So I reasoned that the real thing would have to do for my training ground and the blisters would just have to come and go as they pleased. If I wasn't fit enough, I would become fit as I proceeded. This wouldn't be a prudent strategy for scaling the Himalayas and it proved equally imprudent for el Camino de Santiago de Compostela. What I wasn't ready for was that the day before I departed for Spain, I began to find all sorts of odds and ends that I had neglected to include in my pack, and as a consequence, its weight soared.

Madame Debril.

By the time I was checking in at the airport it tipped the scales at almost 40 pounds—insanely heavy for the ordeal in front of me. But I was a tenderfoot (literally) and would soon realize my mistake and take corrective action.

Madame Debril is an elderly woman, well known, it seems, for stamping pilgrims' credentials when they pass through town. She is very cordial, working out of an office of total clutter. She sits at a large desk by a window and uncovers an oversized journal from the debris to record my visit. I found her by asking several people in town where she lived, all of whom (except the woman running a shop five or six doors away) knew exactly where to send me.

"Where are you starting from?" Madame Debril asks.

"Here," I answer, "from St. Jean Pied-de-Port." This answer doesn't seem to do the trick.

"But where did you come from?" She asks.

"Madrid," she writes in her huge journal.

"I flew from Madrid to Pamplona," I offered in a misguided attempt to clarify the situation.

She writes in her journal again, obviously confused even more. I assume that as a native of the area, it made no sense whatsoever to her for me to travel to St. Jean Pied-de-Port from Pamplona only to walk back to Pamplona. Why not just start in Pamplona like a reasonable person, I'm sure she was thinking. Although not fully settled we mutually decide to let the issue slide and I ask her for a passport, or pilgrims' credential with her official stamp, which all the towns and cities have, to prove that I had in fact passed through. She tells me that she has run out of forms but stamps a piece of paper for me, dates it, and hands it over telling me that I don't need a guidebook, but would do just fine without one. "Follow the yellow arrows," she instructs. "Not the red or white arrows, only the yellow." I put the scrap of paper in my pack, thank her, and head out. She comes outside with me and points the way before striking up a conversation with a passing native.

Yellow arrows leaving St. Jean Pied-de-Port.

The Way led down a cobbled street, through the arch of St. John at the Eglise de Nôtre-Dame, and across a perfect little bridge over the river Nive. Then the trouble begins as the road out of town climbs steeply and passes through a pair of ancient pillars. The trouble being that I am out of shape, carrying an overweight pack, and facing possibly the most difficult portion of the journey. After passing through the pillars, the road continues to climb steeply. I check my watch which tells me I have started much too late to hope to reach Roscesvalles on the Spanish side of the Pyrenees before dark, which in Spain means after 10:30. I continue anyway thinking about the bed and breakfast Madame Debril promised me 5 km out of town. It's a cruel irony of the Camino that the pilgrim faces the Pyrenees on the first day with an overloaded backpack and (in my case) a body accustomed to sitting at a computer. As promised, after 5 km of steady uphill climbing I come to a group of buildings with a sign in French out front, which I take to mean, "Sleep here Carl, you've gone far enough." There is a man working in the garden who directs me inside where a gracious woman who thankfully speaks English tells me that there is no room. The B&B isn't quite what I had expected. As it turns out, it's a posh resort with gourmet cooking where people stay for a week or two enjoying the magnificent scenery.

Bed & breakfast near St. Jean Pied-de-Port.

As I get ready to leave the woman's better judgment must have kicked in (it would be hard to explain a pilgrim found dead of exhaustion on her front step), and she tells me I can sleep in the barn with the sheep and take dinner and breakfast with the guests for a 100 francs. Fortunately I have the money, which is a pure fluke, since my daughter was recently in France and gave me a few hundred francs she returned with. So I am chaperoned up to the barn where there are only four sheep too young to be left outside with the rest of the flock. Paradise in my tired state. I am told I can wait for dinner back at the compound where I go to rearrange my pack, change from my hiking boots into comfortable Reeboks, and sit and watch the sunset. I haven't come far but I feel a lot more confident than I did sitting in the Madrid airport waiting for the plane to Pamplona. I have made a start. It's finally down to the road and me and everything else can wait. After a wonderful four course meal with a dozen other guests, I say good night and head for my barn. Very tired and a little concerned about other critters I might encounter, not including the sheep, I unroll my pad and place my sleeping bag on what seems like a good spot in the middle of the barn. It turns out that the sheep are goats and of the four there is one troublemaker. While three will respond to my suggestion that they sleep in their designated spot, which I promise to respect if they return the favor, the troublemaker needs to inspect the entire new operation that has invaded his space. Only after finding some wood

Rambo Goat.

scraps and building a makeshift fence to keep him in his area, coupled with a few very determined pats with my wooden staff, does Rambo Goat get the idea. Lights out and a well-deserved rest begins when I hear and feel a gentle splat on my sleeping bag. My flashlight reveals a collection of barn swallows perched on the center beam, directly over my spot. The goats decide to investigate now that something interesting is happening and I move my sleeping bag over to the side of the barn and check the overhead structure carefully. Cleaned up and ready to try again after a few more pats with my stick to convince the curious to retire to their end of the barn. Sleep at last—

my first day is over.

June 19
B&B–Roncesvalles

I awake feeling rested and greet my four-legged friends who are getting their noses into everything, including my pack. I pack my gear, say my farewells to my new buddies, and head to the compound for coffee and rolls. As I'm having breakfast, I ask my host if she would be kind enough to mail my tent home for me. I am really desperate to lose some weight and the tent was a terrible idea. After a little persuading and promising to make up for any postage shortage she graciously, though reluctantly, agrees. Thank heavens I can travel about four pounds lighter. After thanking my host for her hospitality, I get myself together and head out, or rather, up. Most of the morning is spent climbing steeply on the narrow country road. After a few km I come to a shepherdess and her dog minding a flock of sheep. As I approach, she stands and murmurs to her dog who has sunk his head down into his haunches and makes growling noises. He is a large German Shepherd who is very anxious to prove he can protect the sheep in his care, and his growling has a curious pleading quality, which I interpret as—"Please let me eat this pilgrim. He looks like a menace to the world." The shepherdess whispered to him: "Leave this one alone and I promise you can eat the next one that passes." We exchange bonjours, and I trudge passed them and around a bend. A little way further I come to a very curious statue of the Virgin Mary holding a headless Christ child. It seems a little odd that someone would steal the head of Christ, but I suppose that reliquary thieves are atheists and have no fear of divine retribution.

Mary with headless child.

After a short rest, I continue on the now gently climbing road noticing the numerous shooting blinds hunters have built for the migrating birds who take this route south. Rain is threatening and I make sure I have my poncho ready for action in its pocket on top of my pack. When I reach what I hope is the very top of the pass, heavy rain with accompanying wind begins and I whip out my rain poncho for the first time and struggle trying to figure out its system of snaps, fighting the strong wind. The poncho is designed to cover the pack and me, and I'm glad there is no one around since I must look like a dog chasing his tail trying to get the thing on properly in the wind and rain. Finally I am successful and after about twenty paces the rain stops

Looking back.

abruptly. Good practice, I tell myself, and continue for half an hour or so before taking off the poncho, folding it up, and replacing it in its pocket on my pack. I bumped into several groups of hikers; some started from St. Jean in France and hike to Roncesvalles and back as a day trip. Others drive part way up then walk to the French-Spanish border and back. As I continue on a few km, it becomes obvious that I am nowhere near the top of the pass, and the road becomes enshrouded in a heavy fog, beautiful and mysterious. I hear singing and laughing and suddenly a group of schoolgirls appear out of the fog a few feet in front of me. I am busy photographing the beechwood trees wrapped in mist as we greet each other briefly and continue our separate ways. The road remains flat for a while, and I pass the marker for the frontier before it begins gently sloping downward through the forest. Soon I emerge onto a rougher road that looks like it has been excavated recently for a construction project and begins to climb again. It's not a steep climb,

Frontier marker.

but for me it's difficult and seemingly unending. It's late afternoon, and as I struggle up the hills with my heavy pack, I find I have to stop frequently and rest since I'm getting worn out already. Actually, I'm exhausted and hoping the upward part of the journey will end soon. Now and then a pilgrim or two would pass me and we'd usually exchange a few words. I could see the concern about me in their eyes, and the hope that the pathetic creature I've become will wait to drop dead until they get over the next rise. I am beginning to have serious doubts about my ability to complete this pilgrimage if

The summit.

my current difficulty is any indication of what's to come. My resolve is high, however, and I know that I must make it to the monastery at Roncesvalles before nightfall, so I trudge onward and upward. At long last, I reach what seems to be the summit at Lepoeder where the dirt road meets a paved road. I put down my pack and take a few photographs, but it's bleak and distinctly anticlimactic since the summit is large and mostly flat with no commanding vistas. A Land Rover with four men crawls up the paved road, engine groaning in low gear, and takes a cart path up towards the top of an adjoining rise.

Thankfully, the path takes a turn and begins the decent to Roncesvalles

3.5 km away, according to my guidebook. Going down isn't the relaxing piece of cake I thought it would be. Did I mention that I was tired? I am thankful for the walking stick I bought in St. Jean Pied-de-Port since it is very helpful negotiating the sometimes treacherous ruts in the path. Going down uses an entirely different set of muscles than when climbing and after about one km my legs really begin to feel it, in addition to the blisters that are forming. The dirt path through the forest is very beautiful, though,

Forest on the decent.

and near the bottom I begin to hear voices and can't help wondering if I am hallucinating. As I progress slowly along the path, step-by-step, and feeling every inch, I turn to find two young men a few feet behind me. They are walking briskly, talking, and showing no signs of fatigue whatsoever. Ah, youth. For them this is like a stroll in the park, while I am inching along in what is probably the most torturous physical endurance test of my life. Polite greetings and they're gone. Eventually, I come to my first sighting of the Roncesvalles building complex with its uncharacteristic metal roofs on the otherwise ancient edifices. After crossing a small stream, I enter the grounds from the back and walk along the rather stately and well-kept grounds to the building where I am registered and my pilgrim's passport is stamped. Since Madame Dubril didn't have a proper pilgrim credential, the officiating priest prepared one for me with the appropriate stamps. The German youths who passed me on the road registered at the same time.

Signing in.

As part of the signing in, pilgrims are asked to fill out a form that asks the reasons you are embarking on the pilgrimage. The choices are: religious, spiritual, cultural, or other, with a check box for each. I check off spiritual and return the form that looks like a Xerox in its thousandth generation of replication. We get the rundown on the rules:

1. Find a bunk in the Refugio (dorm)
2. Mass at eight (in about an hour)
3. Dinner in the restaurant on the grounds (pilgrim discount)
4. Lights out at ten
5. Sleep
6. Up and out by eight in the morning.

The sleeping area is on the third and top floor of an ancient building adjacent to the church. I was a little apprehensive since I had never stayed in a youth hostel before and didn't quite know what to expect. My previous experiences with communal living were Boy Scout Camp at age thirteen,

Hostel and Collegiate Church.

and first year at college where, due to a shortage of rooms, I was placed in a large room with five other students for several weeks. Both were situations where you needed to stay alert and defensive to avoid falling prey to a prankster or some other mischief. Once up on the top floor, I entered a common room with a long table. There are notices and posters relating to pilgrim life on the walls and the showers and bathrooms are on your left. At the end of the room on the right is the door to the sleeping area that is one large room filled with double decker bunk beds. I entered the room and was put at ease

Sleeping quarters.

immediately by the calm, relaxed atmosphere of everyone; men and women were going about their business of unpacking and finding what they needed for washing up, changing clothes, and socializing with one another. I selected a lower bunk and spread out my sleeping bag, found my towel and a clean shirt and had a shower. Everything went along smoothly. After getting settled in, I decide to walk down to the gift shop/bar in search of a phone to call my wife, Cameron. I find the phone alright, but can't seem to make it respond to an international call, nor can the bartender. Sitting at a table there is a single customer who speaks English and intervenes as translator on my behalf, but in the end we all decide that the phone simply isn't wired for international calls and give it up. Meanwhile, the Good Samaritan and I introduce ourselves and have a brief conversation. Turns out he is Howard from Australia, who arrived yesterday or the day before. He advises me to scurry up to the restaurant before Mass and put in my reservation for the discounted pilgrim dinner. Somehow these instructions passed me by as I was checking in, which is no surprise since the priest spoke mostly Spanish. I rush up to the restaurant and duly place a reservation just in time to make the Mass. Mind you, I'm not Catholic, nor even a practicing Episcopalian as I was raised, but I reasoned that attending the Mass was in some way my payback for the free room and in my condition, well worth the price. Actually, I had never attended a full-fledged Catholic Mass before and was looking forward to the experience. The 13th century Collegiate Church was quite full as I entered a few minutes late. While I recognized some of the pilgrims from the Refugio, most of the congregation consisted of visitors and people from the community. I really didn't know quite what to expect, but as the Mass progressed I was very moved by the beauty of the altar with its roof supported by four posts, and the singsong chanting of the priest. Near the end of the Mass, the pilgrims were asked to step forward and approach the altar for a special blessing. Speaking very little Spanish and less Latin, I didn't understand a word that was spoken but simply followed the other pilgrims. As it turned out, while I was to attend many Masses in some very fine and ancient cathedrals before my pilgrimage was over, this was one of the most beautiful. Perhaps it was the novelty for me, but I felt that the quality of the organ music as well as the priest's talent for the job, and the feeling of community with the congregation all worked together to make this Mass stand out.

Mass in Collegiate Church.

The dinner was at the restaurant across the compound and directly on the road. There was a single table of pilgrims. Howard, the Australian I met earlier in the bar, was there along with Sune and Henrietta, a young Danish couple, Manuel, a Spaniard, and Tim, another Australian. Here we all were, thrown together as strangers to enjoy a meal together before continuing our journey. Tim, it turns out, is a very outgoing adventurer who likes to travel when he isn't working as a foreman on a diamond mining crew. He was on a tour bus when it stopped in Roncesvalles, one of the scheduled sights. When he saw the pilgrims with backpacks milling around he asked the driver about it and learned about the Camino de Santiago. He had never heard of it before but decided right then and there that it was more interesting than his tour bus, so he got off and instantly became a pilgrim. He had a backpack and hiking boots with him so he was perfectly equipped, making the decision easier. The other Australian, Howard, was older, in his late forties, and quite a character. He told us he was a freelance writer, photographer, and teacher. He had traveled quite a bit and oddly, he did not have an Australian accent. When I first met him earlier, I took him for an American. He told us that he had a very difficult time crossing the Pyrenees and almost required medical treatment for his ailing legs and feet. He had arrived a day or two earlier and was resting before going on tomorrow. He announced that he was planning to walk at a leisurely pace and invited anyone who was interested in joining him to meet at his hotel in the next town in the morning for coffee. Tim and I agreed to do so. Sune was doing graduate work in political science, preparing for a career as an environmentalist, and Henrietta was a nurse studying to become a midwife. Manuel was a student from Madrid. The menu was a choice between meat or fish, with wine and a vegetable. The fish was great, especially since I hadn't eaten since breakfast at the B&B that morning. We chatted a bit, enjoyed each other's company, but couldn't linger very long since the Refugio's ten o'clock curfew was coming hard upon us. As I settled into my sleeping bag, the man in charge of keeping the Refugio running smoothly urged everyone to settle down as he turned out the light.

June 20

Roncesvalles–Zubiri

The next morning the hostelero at Roncesvalles has everyone hustling to be out the door by 8 A.M. sharp. He is a stocky man in his mid-forties with an air of terse politeness. Pilgrims socializing as they pack are encouraged not to dally, as the hostel must be cleaned up and ready for those arriving today. As I came to learn very soon, every Refugio has its own style of operation determined by the volunteers who run it. The volunteers are always seasoned pilgrims themselves who feel especially connected to the Camino and wish to give something back. Some Refugios are run with a no-nonsense military attitude while others are more relaxed. But even the most relaxed Refugios have you on the road bright and early, and nothing short of a doctor's word will get you more than a single night. Every Refugio has a doctor or clinic on call, free of charge to any pilgrim carrying a certified pilgrim credential, the passport that is stamped at every Refugio as you progress along the Camino. While some Refugios have paid caretakers who run the place on a more or less permanent basis, most have volunteers who work for a few weeks before moving on. More often than not the volunteers are not Spanish, but represent the entire spectrum of pilgrim nationalities.

Outside the hostel I met up with the Australian, Tim, and we set off towards Burguete, the next town, 3.9 km away. It was a clear invigorating morning and we took to the road at rapid pace set by Tim. Fortunately the road was flat, but right away I knew I was in trouble trying to keep the pace. Every bone in my body was creaking from yesterday's ordeal, while Tim, who was just beginning his pilgrimage, was fresh as a daisy. Not wanting to sound like a weenie on my third day as a pilgrim, I kept the pace while filling Tim in on the miracle of St. James. The fact that he knew nothing at all about why pilgrims were taking this route made his impromptu decision to join us even more impressive. As we walked into Burguete, we passed a bar where the German lads were having beer for breakfast and marveled at their stamina. The town itself was clean and tidy, but a bit austere. Somewhere near the center of town, a few hundred meters in, we located Howard's hotel and found him finishing breakfast in the dining room. The hotel was exactly like the town, clean and proper. The waiter asked Tim and I to move our packs out to the entrance hall while we ate breakfast. We ordered coffee and some pastry and chatted with Howard, who was looking at his guidebook and discussing the road ahead. Behind us on the wall hung a newspaper clipping with a photograph of Ernest Hemingway writing in the very room we were in. Very impressive and a huge claim to fame for the hotel, I'm sure. We got ourselves together and walked out to the narrow sidewalk and along the main street. Just before the Camino broke off to the right, we came upon the church of San Nicolás de Bari where I stopped to photograph the beautiful San Nicolás de Bari Baroque portal.

San Nicolás de Bari.

Tim and Howard lingered a moment but were more interested in walking and continued on. When I finished and started to walk I could see them up ahead engaged in conversation and walking at the same quick pace set by Tim. I worried about Howard because of what he had told us about the physical difficulty he had crossing the Pyrenees and having to rest for a day before continuing, and I knew from earlier in the morning that Tim's pace was too quick for me so I decided not to try and catch up. That was the last I was to see of either of them. My concern for Howard was well founded since I heard later from the Danish couple, Sune and Henrietta, that Howard had to take another more extended break since he had developed serious blisters that day. Not just ordinary blisters, but blisters with blood in them, and also that he was determined to finish the pilgrimage even if it took him until September. As I continued to walk through the countryside, and after passing a few towns, the road began to rise steeply to the Alto de Erro.

El Camino.

This is Charlemagne country. It was in Burguete that Roland, Oliveros, and King Marsilius (the Moorish caliph) were defeated in battle along with

40,000 Christian and Saracen soldiers. Legend holds it was the Basques in collusion with the Moors who attacked Charlemagne's rear guard, commanded by Roland. As I climbed the steep trail, winding through brambles, hazel, and beech trees, I came across the famous stone known as Roland's footstep, which is about two meters long. A good thing it has a sign on it, I thought, since I undoubtedly would have walked right by it.

Roland's Footstep.

I was becoming more fatigued with every passing km, and less and less attentive to the environment. Eventually, after a difficult trek, I came upon the Venta del Puerto (Inn of the Pass). In and around the building, which is now a cowshed, a herd of fine looking golden brown cows, who are grazing startled me a bit since they sported very sharp looking horns and didn't seem to appreciate my sudden appearance. After deciding that I wasn't a threat, they lost their curiosity in me and went about their business.

Venta del Puerto.

Through an opening in the trees, I could see an industrial plant far in the distance spewing a thick cloud of white smoke over the entire valley it occupied. Hoping that the plant wasn't my destination for the day since it looked much too far away, I decided to stop and have lunch. I didn't have a guidebook yet so I really wasn't sure about my destination. I'd lost the guidebook I bought in Pamplona that was in Spanish anyway and of limited use to me. All I had was a couple of Energizer Bars that I had brought all the way from home and water. By this time, I was really quite tired and appreciated the rest, and what more fitting place than an ancient inn. It was about 12 noon and after about half an hour I struggled to my feet, bid adiós to the cows, and continued. Like the day before, the downward walk turned out to be the real challenge. Not only because the way became seriously steep and rutted with loose stones, but also because it is at the end of the day when I am most tired. Now, as it would many more times as I continued, the Camino became a true test of endurance. My overweight pack was becoming a more of a burden and my spirits were starting to deplete along with my water supply.

Factory at Zubiri.

El Camino seemed endless, but there was no choice but to walk on. Although it wasn't really that far (about 4 km) from Venta del Puerto to Zubiri, which was to be my destination, it seemed a lot further because of the very rough terrain and my poor condition. Finally, I came to a clearing and see that the cement plant with its billowing smoke stacks is indeed my destination, and soon walk out of the hillside and onto the paved streets of the town of Zubiri. After crossing the bridge which seemed unremarkable to my weary eyes, despite the fact that the Zubiri means "village of the bridge" in Basque, and the bridge has two Gothic arches, I came to the main street and asked directions to the Refugio. I was directed to turn right and continue down a bit where I would find it on the left side of the road. Zubiri is not an especially picturesque town as Spanish towns go. It is built on the river Arga which runs parallel to the main street and the town is dominated by the cement factory at the west end. In fact, the factory dominates the whole of the immediate river valley, which is responsible for the polluted air billowing from its smoke stacks. Lots of construction is going on to put up mini high rises, and with the exception of the bridge, not much to see of architectural interest. The whole town has the appearance of having been built within the last decade or so. This being my first Refugio except for Roncesvalles, which you couldn't miss, I must admit I had some difficulty identifying it. As instructed, I walked down the main street and first looked at what seemed like a high-rise condo, which clearly wasn't a Refugio. The next set of buildings had a playground for youngsters in front of it with long buildings going away from the road. Obvious as it must have been to any seasoned pilgrim, I remained baffled and walked down to the end building and opened the door to find a gymnasium. Feeling the full impact of being a confused foreigner, and realizing that I had no idea what to expect, or what a Refugio actually looks like, I cautiously went to the next doorway which had doors on the left and right of an open shower-room door. This looked very promising, but the left hand door was locked. I opened the door on the right and entered a room filled with bunk beds and a single patron sleeping on a lower bunk at the far end. At last, refuge for a weary pilgrim. On the wall just inside the door was a drop box for donations: 200 pesetas (about $1.50). The room was about 30 feet long and 12 feet wide with windows and a long table on one side and bunk beds lining the other long wall and the end walls. I entered, selected a lower bunk nearest the door and unpacked my gear in preparation for a shower. After taking a shower and returning to the bunkhouse, my fellow pilgrim was stirring and we soon discovered that we had no language in common. He was French and spoke a little Spanish but no English, and I spoke no French. He was to be known thereafter as the French Guy. Since relationships on the Camino are fleeting, people were usually reduced to their most salient characteristic in lieu of proper names. There was the American couple, the Norwegian couple, etc. I learned later that the French Guy was also known as Mr. Quick because he walked very fast. So there we were reduced to pantomiming but able to communicate surprisingly well. We motioned and groaned about the difficulty of the last bit of Camino, and then the subject of food came up and we decided to investigate the possibilities. My new companion was a short, balding man in his late fifties with a tanned complexion. I decided to go out and call home at a phone booth a few meters up the street. When I returned to the Refugio, the French Guy was outside talking to a native in French. I couldn't believe it. Just by chance, in the middle of Spain, the French Guy finds someone who speaks fluent French. Turns out the French Guy is very excitable and is in a perfect snit. His guidebook indicated that there would be a restaurant nearby and open, and the native has informed him otherwise. I suggested we find a bar, which seemed like a stroke of genius to my new friend, and he proceeded to chat with the native about this idea. Apparently satisfied with the native's response about the whereabouts of a suitable bar, we set off down the road to the center of town about 400 meters away, but not before he cautioned me not to leave any money at the Refugio. The bar turned out to be a small, husband and wife market where we bought food for dinner and had our credentials stamped by the proprietors. Being a novice pilgrim, I followed the lead of the French Guy in buying some blood sausage, an item seen hanging in any market but one that, for some reason, I had never associated with food. We also bought oranges, canned peppers, wine, cheese, and bread. I bought a couple of cans of Naranja (orange drink), which I was becoming addicted to. I knew I was also buying tomorrow's lunch. We walked back to the Refugio and ate our sumptuous dinner at the long table. During dinner the French Guy told me that not only was this his third pilgrimage, but that he'd had triple bypass surgery. He pulled open his shirt to reveal a huge scar running down the center of his chest, and then pulled up his pant leg to reveal another scar where they had taken an artery. I was very impressed. Since I hadn't eaten all day, the meal was extraordinarily good. The combination of canned peppers, oranges, and blood sausage was totally new for me. After dinner, we cleaned up the table and I set about washing my socks, underwear, and T-shirt in preparation for the next day's walk. I hung my clothes out to dry on one of the playground's fixtures, a circular ride made of iron bars, which made a perfect clothesline. I was finally beginning to feel human again and the French Guy suggested we go back to town for coffee, which I agreed to. We found a little bar that seemed to double as a teen center where we sat down at a table and ordered coffee above the very loud music. We both ordered café solo which was served by a waitress who was doing her best to hold back a laughing fit. I have no idea what exactly, about the two foreigners, struck her as so funny. I don't think the French Guy noticed and we enjoyed our café solo in the disco and walked back to the Refugio.

The French Guy and I were sitting on the stoop and it was beginning to get dark when the French Girl arrived, walking alone, deep in her own world. She was in her mid-thirties, slim and attractive, and, like the French Guy, well-tanned. We all greeted each other and she went in after a brief conversation with the French Guy and myself. She spoke English as well as French. I was glad to see another pilgrim arrive since, while the French Guy and I were getting along well enough, the language barrier is like a wall that takes a little getting used to. Shortly afterwards, the American couple, Ron and Linda, arrived. Both were short and stocky and looked as though they could hike anywhere. They were carrying huge packs and looked tired. Ron immediately asked, "Who's in charge?" "I am," I responded. Obviously he didn't believe me because he asked again and I told him about the honor system and the locked drop box inside. They entered and settled in. After about half an hour, the French Cyclists showed up. They were doing a whirlwind pilgrimage and expected to be in Santiago de Compostela inside of two weeks. Everyone proceeded their thing, showering, clothes washing, and sitting around chatting. The nearly empty Refugio had suddenly turned into a bustling hostel with pilgrims talking and laughing while they prepared for the night's rest and the next day's challenges.

June 21
Zubiri–Pamplona

The French Guy is gone. Everyone else is busy packing and I am working on a letter and thinking about how I'm going to mail a package home with the unnecessary stuff I am carrying. After yesterday's walk I am determined to lighten up my load, both physically and spiritually. Watching the others pack and talk among themselves, it's easy for me to feel the self-conscious brooding that can be like a cloak I wear. In a blink of an eye, it can turn into fear and insecurity. While packing, I talk with Ron and Linda for a few minutes. Turns out that they had a difficult day yesterday. Linda has back problems and Ron helps her out frequently by portaging her heavy pack up the more difficult parts of the trail. Although this makes for slow going they are in good spirits and I feel a kinship with these fellow Americans. After finishing my own packing, I head off towards town in search of coffee and a post office. I stopped in a bar and ordered café solo from a distinctly cool proprietor. The coffee was good as usual, and after finishing I walked a few doors down to where I learned the post office was in a hostel. Zubiri, being a bustling community with a large factory, must, I reasoned, have a decent post office. How would people mail packages to friends and family in other regions otherwise? After entering the tiny lobby and confirming with the woman behind the counter that this was indeed the post office, with my usual pathetic Spanish and pantomiming, I explained that I wanted to mail a package home. Her response eluded me for the most part, and after a while she summoned her husband from the back room. Eventually, it became very clear that I could send letters but a package was out of the question, especially a package that didn't exist. I needed to find a box and then wrapping paper

Factory grounds.

and string. Ok, live and learn. I knew the idea of mailing a package was going to be a mission, so after eating a croissant that appeared out of nowhere, I started the day's journey. I would be carrying my heavy load for some time to come. Someone along the way suggested that an enterprising native could make a good living specializing in arranging to have all the useless stuff pilgrims start out with sent home. I'm sure it's true. As I left the post office and started down the street, I caught a glimpse of Ron and Linda a few hundred meters away headed back in the direction of the Refugio. Too, far away to hail them, I hoped that they were ok, since they were not heading out on the Camino. That was the last I was to see of them. Back over the bridge, I fend off a couple of unchained guard dogs as the owners half-heartedly call them back, and trudge through the grim landscape of the factory grounds. From the hill overlooking the factory, I could see the valley stretching out below

Note.

and the road where cyclists, like the French group who stayed at the Refugio last night, were moving at a fast pace. I was glad to be away from the traffic, on foot, alone. Just before entering the luscious path that followed the river Arga, I came upon a note on a marker left in the hope that the intended recipient would pass by and read it. I thought of all the fleeting relationships formed on the Camino, and the sweet futility of this message. How often have we formed brief relationships, in which things were left unsaid only to regret the mistake later.

I found this section of the Camino very refreshing. Walking next to a river and smelling and hearing its life undoubtedly had a relaxing effect. The path is narrow and just a few feet from the fast moving river. At one point a cyclist came up behind me and asked if I had seen the rest of his group. I hadn't, but a few km further on, where the Camino joined the highway for a bit, I came upon the group. At about noon, I stopped for lunch in Larrasoaña. While I sat eating my sausage, bread, and cheese, the old man of the village (every village has a few of these ancient sentries) told me it was going to rain. After climbing a hill to Zuriáin, I met an old farmer who spoke at length about his relatives who had moved to the United States. I was unable to confirm the rain prediction, and as yet there was no sign of water from the sky.

At about 4:30, I stopped to rest at a bridge and watched some kids washing their car for a while before continuing. By this time I was exhausted. No kick left, but the section is a steep climb. In the distance coming up behind me, I saw two pilgrims and I thought, oh good, here come Ron and Linda, and while they turned out to be an American couple, they weren't who I thought they were. We met at the top of a steep climb where the path leveled off for awhile around the base of a hill. They were Carson and Anna who I was to bump into off and on several times during our pilgrimage. Again, it was a real treat to be able to talk with people from home, and compare a few

Trinidad de Arre.

notes on our impressions as well as to complain a little about the difficulty. Anna was having serious problems with her feet, and like Ron, Carson was helping her by portaging her pack up some of the steeper climbs. I was very impressed with the strength and stamina of these guys, climbing the roughest hills twice. They told me that Pamplona was about 10 km ahead. At this point I didn't have a guidebook and was glad to hear that I was closing in on my destination. On I went while they rested for a while. This last few km to Pamplona and the following day turned out to be the most difficult for me. More difficult than crossing the Pyrenees and even more difficult than climbing to Foncebadón and the Iron Cross, which marks the highest point of the Camino later on. This was due to my as yet unconditioned body and the unrelenting routine of walking hard every day without rest. It was getting to me, but there was little choice but to walk. I had severe blisters on my heels that simply couldn't heal as long as I continued to walk, but walking was why I had come, so walk I did. At about 6:30, I was finally approaching Pamplona, the city I had flown into three days earlier. As I approached from the East I could see the walls of the city and it seemed as though it would not get closer. Here was a city founded by the Roman general Pomey around 75 B.C., but I could care less since every step required a supreme act of will. I had pushed myself beyond my physical limit and I was concerned that if I stopped for more than a moment, I would not be able to summon the courage or will to force my body to move. I was walking like an ancient traveler, every step considered, slow and measured. Time stopped. All that was left was the next step and the pain. After walking past the walls and up the steps to the city, I entered a street with dingy nightclubs and loud music. My greeting to Pamplona was the drunken patrons of the nightclubs, lingering at the doorways and spilling into the street, loud and boisterous, sneering and yelling nasty remarks as I limped past. I was sure I had just arrived in

Hell. Having lost track of the yellow arrows, I eventually entered a square in the old section with no idea whatsoever where to find the Refugio. St. James smiled upon me, however, and in what appears to be a fantastic coincidence, with hundreds of people milling around, I encountered Sune and Henrietta who directed me to the Refugio located close-by on the third floor of an ancient church. The Refugio is in the old section of Pamplona where I had never ventured on my first visit, since I was so intent on reaching St. Jean Pied-de-Port. I rang the bell for the intercom and was buzzed in. The sleeping quarters were three floors up a winding staircase and I thought I would die climbing the stairs hauling my heavy pack. When finally I made it, a group of three kindly old men were running the place, none of whom spoke English. I was able to learn, however, that the doors close at 9:30. This earlier than usual closing time created a problem for anyone interested in eating dinner in a restaurant, none of which serve before 9:00, not leaving enough time to eat. After showering and washing my socks and a couple of shirts, I ventured out in search of food. Although I certainly could have gone for a good meal, I decided instead to have tapas (various finger foods) and wine at a local bar. After returning to the Refugio just before it closed, I spoke with Sune and Henrietta for a few minutes before going to sleep. Henrietta had blisters and I introduced her to a method I had read about of bursting the blister with a sterile needle and a short piece of thread. The thread is pulled through the blister and left in place in order to allow the liquid to wick out and prevent the blister from closing up again and continuing to be a problem. The noise from the street was very loud since there was a festival in progress, and I heard later that some people just left in the middle of the night rather than trying to fight it. The Spanish know how to party. At this hour the paseo is in full swing, with families and young adults mingling with boisterous teens in the streets. With hundreds of people out to enjoy themselves the noise is deafening. Impromptu bands erupt every few minutes adding to the mayhem yet no one seems to become violent and no one is threatened. My impression is that this could never happen in America. There appears to be a social code of conduct here by which everyone conducts themselves, drunk or sober, and which disallows threatening others or destroying property. In my experience, when Americans congregate and drink, they inevitably become rowdy, violent, and destructive.

June 22
Pamplona–Puente La Reina

I left before dawn the next morning while most of the pilgrims still slept. I really should have spent a little more time in Pamplona to look around the historic city and give myself the opportunity to eat a decent breakfast. I didn't realize how exhausted I was from the last couple of days of hard walking, and, as it turned out, I had a difficult walk ahead of me this day. As I began walking through Pamplona it was still dark and the only signs of life were the revelers winding down from the night's festivities. The cars that were out often honked in a menacing manner as they streaked past

Ahead: Santa María de Erreniega.

with kids. At this early hour there were no bars open in the section of town I was walking through. I was quite famished and hated to see the city fall behind before even a cup of coffee came my way. As I walked on past Cizur on my right, I eventually began a trek through a gently sloping plain which led to the Alto de Santa Maria de Erreniega. This is one of the highest points of Sierra del Perdón, where a row of impressive wind turbines is whirling away. Climbing this hill after half a day's walk with no food and little water severely taxed my physical endurance. I felt like a mountain goat

Sculpture and Pamplona Basin.

making my way up the narrow path. Resting frequently, weighted down by my heavy pack, many pilgrims passed me looking very concerned about my condition. When finally reaching the summit, I looked back in amazement to see the Pamplona basin I had just traversed with the Pyrenees Mountains in the background. When I turned and looked in the other direction I realized that I would be walking as far as the eye could see before reaching my destination: Puente La Reina. I took photographs of the landscape and an amazing contemporary steel sculpture of a band of pilgrims with the huge windmills whirring away behind me. Talking to another American later, he told me that he was so exhausted at this point that he became ill and vomited

Giant windmills.

before continuing. Here I was, only five days into my pilgrimage feeling very unfit and genuinely concerned about my prospects of completing the journey. Nevertheless, after resting for a while, I hoisted my pack up on my shoulders and continued down the treacherously rutted and stony path on the other side of the summit. Eventually, I entered the town of Uterga, which seemed like a sizable place—certainly big enough to have a bar or restaurant I thought. But as fate would have it there was no such place, only a fountain for which I was grateful. At about 2:30 in the afternoon I dragged into the next town, Muruzábal, and immediately entered the bar. I had been walking since dawn, mostly in the hot sun, and hadn't eaten since the tapas in Pamplona the previous night. The bar in Muruzábal was, of course, in the main plaza, and I wearily made my way to a table in the back beyond the bar populated by several natives. Children came and went noisily, and a couple of old men ate at the table in front of me. After putting down my pack, I went to the bar and ordered a café solo and a couple of tapas (485 Pts.) that I took back to my table. This was turning out to be more of an ordeal by starvation. I resolved to try and be more cautious and carry more food and water. Two days of physical hardship had depleted my energy more than I realized. All the more so when insufficient nourishment is added to the mix.

At 4:30, I arrived in Puente La Reina and entered the crowded bunkhouse of the Refugio. There were at least thirty bunks, triple-decker, jammed into the small "L" shaped room. After selecting a bunk and washing my clothes, I went to the main building to check in and get my pilgrim's credential stamped. Business taken care of, I entered the 12th century Iglesia del

Portal of Iglesia del Crucifijo.

Crucifijo to experience the famous German crucifix from which the church gets its name. This crucifix is very powerful and I sat feeling its energy for some time. Eventually I ventured out into the rather large and spread-out town and explored it a bit, had a beer and tapas, and headed back to the Refugio. Before turning in, I spoke with a young Norwegian couple who were doing the Camino at an accelerated pace. They told me of a pilgrimage of sorts in Norway from Oslo into the mountains. Not one of a religious nature like the Camino de Santiago, which we were on, but one appreciated for its natural and pristine beauty. I asked them if they had seen the American couple I left in Zubiri and they said they had, but I wasn't convinced it was the same couple, and still worried about them.

June 23
Puente La Reina–Estella

This morning I found a guidebook in English. I have been looking for one since Roncesvalles where I first learned of their existence. I bought a Spanish guidebook in Pamplona and had been using it until I lost it somewhere along the way. It was somewhat useful, but since I don't read (or speak) Spanish, only the map part of the guidebook was of value. I left my pack with my wallet in it back at the Refugio, so I asked the storekeeper to hold the guidebook and a few postcards for me until I returned. Back at the Refugio, I noticed that someone had picked up the air mattress and sweatshirt that I left in the previous town, Obanos, and left it on the table at the Refugio. Naturally, they were thinking they were doing a good deed and helping out a careless pilgrim. In fact, I left the items to shed a little weight, which I was becoming painfully aware of with every kilometer. I supposed that this was a sign that I wasn't spiritually prepared to lighten up yet. The idea of leaving behind physical objects as a symbol of lightening up spiritually appealed to me and I decided to continue to leave a little something behind occasionally as a conscious reinforcement. I decided to give it another try and just left the stuff on the table and returned to the shop to buy the guidebook and postcards. At 10 A.M. after café solo and croissants, I am finally leaving Puenta la Reina. I stopped at a market and bought bread and cheese for lunch, not wanting to repeat the starvation ordeal of yesterday. The market had a large poster of St. James on the wall that made me feel

Leaving Puenta la Reina.

good. Halfway down the street, I realized that I left my walking stick behind and just as I turned to go back, the shopkeeper came running up to me with it. I thanked him profusely and continued, feeling the weight of my heavy pack. It is perfect day—about 70 degrees, with bright sun on the low hills of wheat. At a turn in the path, I came upon a bag of small pears opened very invitingly. After considering for a few seconds, I decided to accept the

Gift of pears

invitation and eat one, even though I wasn't hungry. I could sense that someone had placed the offering with great deliberation. It tasted sweet and was very refreshing. I silently thanked whoever had left them as I walked on. Gratitude, I have learned, is a significant part of the learning and spiritual growth process. It helps to neutralize negativity and points out the positive aspects of life as the result of grace rather than ego-driven achievement.

At the top of a steep path, I came to the ruins of the Hospital de Bargota, according to my new guidebook, which I could finally read, and reinforced by a large sign proclaiming the spot. As I looked around, however, I saw no ruins. All I could detect that could even remotely be taken for ruins was a pile of rocks a few feet away from where I was standing. I thought that

Hospital de Bargota.

labeling this pile of rocks as a cultural site was really going too far with the celebration of the historic. I selected a small one to bring home to Cameron, took a photograph, and walked on. The black flies were becoming very annoying and the soles of my feet hurt badly. Just after the village of Cirauqui, I stopped at a Roman bridge to rest. I hoped to make it to Estella by the end of the day, a distance of about 22 km (13 miles). Not very far, but considering the terrain and my condition, making it remained an open question. Eventually, as I continued to walk, I began to feel a little better than I had the first few days, which were filled with fear and uncertainty when I spent time playing back old movies in my head of imaginary mistakes and regrets causing the path to be both spiritually and physically torturous. The voice of the self-recriminator seems always to be ready to take control if he is allowed.

Ancient Roman bridge.

As I emerged from a bushy trail, I came upon a chair placed in the center of a clearing— a simple chrome tube kitchen type of chair. I take this to be another invitation like the pears in the path earlier, so I sit for a while and admire the view. At 3:30, after trudging up a hill, I stop for lunch in a cozy little rose garden in front of the Church of San Salvador at Lorca. Except for the dogs barking constantly, it was a pleasant place. 4.5 km further on, I came to Villatuerta and its imposing church, Iglesia La Asunción, huge, with walls shaped and reinforced much like a bunker of some sort.

Iglesia La Asunción.

Something about it made me cringe. After walking a few more km, on a hill overlooking the village, I came upon another bunker type building that to me resembled the church very closely and confirmed my suspicions about the ominous appearance of the church. This newer and smaller building

Ominous architecture.

was very mysterious. I have no idea what its purpose was and there was no signage. The bunker had no windows and concrete ribbed sides very much like the church—frightening really. I couldn't help thinking that something sinister was afoot in both structures.

I arrived in Estella at 6:30. The Refugio in Estella is modern, clean, and run by a man who hates pilgrims, which has a seriously dampening effect on the welcoming experience. Upon checking in, you are asked to sign up for the breakfast he provides for an additional 500 Pts. The breakfast is a rip off, consisting of fruit and a variety of packaged pastries. After selecting my bunk, I performed the daily ritual of washing my socks and shirt as soon as possible so they will have the maximum time to dry before I leave in the morning. The room has tiny balconies outside the windows from which I can find a spot to hang my laundry to dry. My laundry duties done, I venture out to explore the town and find some food. Estella is a very picturesque town with Río Ega running through it, spanned by a couple of quaint little bridges. I crossed one of the bridges and ran into a group of Americans who were on their way to dinner. It turned out they were guiding a small group of students over part of the camino, and invited me to join them at the restaurant where they had made reservations. The dinner consisted of a couple of paper-thin pork chops, soup, and wine. We had an interesting conversation about the nature of Art and photography since a couple of the students were studying photography. After learning that I teach photography in Boston, one of the students asked me if I considered photography Art. I responded that the question had been settled in photography's favor decades ago and that the question of Art or not Art is not determined in any way by the medium an individual is working in, but rather by the ideas and attitudes that motivate the individual.

Estella.

June 24
Estella–Los Arcos

Leaving Estella.

As I walked out of Estella, I came to an ancient gate. Before passing through, I stopped and looked at the high rises on the other side and felt a distinct reluctance to pass from an ancient world into a contemporary one. No choice—I had to keep walking. As in Puente la Reina, I felt a need to leave a little something behind, so after speaking with two horses who were corralled in a small lot overlooking the city, I gave them an apple and left a small scallop shell that had been given to me by my friend Jackie who lives on Cape Cod. She had given me a small collection before I left and I pinned one to my hat as a symbol of my pilgrimage.

The legend of El Camino de Santiago de Compostela includes the story of a bridegroom who was drowned when he and the horse he was riding were swept into the sea as he was riding along the beach to his wedding. When his bride appealed to Saint James the groom arose from the sea covered with shells. From then on the scallop shell became the mark of all who fought the infidel and the badge of those who make the pilgrimage. Most pilgrims have a scallop shell sewn or hanging from their pack and it is incorporated into much of the architecture along the route as an ornamental element.

Wine or water.

Before long, I arrived at Irache where there is a very unusual fountain provided by a winery from which visitors have a choice between wine or water. Although it is only 11:30 I of course sample the wine, which tasted very bitter to me and I hoped it wasn't the best they could produce. Despite my negative assessment, I took a half-liter for later in order to give it a "fair chance." Later I ran into a group of young Germans who raved about it and filled their water bottles with the free wine. A few paces up the hill is the amazing Irache Monastery where the guard allowed me to pass without paying the entrance fee.

Monastery of Irache Cloisters.

Records of the monastery go back as far as 958 but the current Romanesque church on the site was completed in the 13th century.

Although the parking lot outside was teaming with tour groups and their huge busses, I was the only visitor inside and grateful for the opportunity to experience its powerful energy in solitude. Despite the fact that I am not Catholic, I felt a particular affinity to this church and its beautiful cloisters. The ancient architects knew how to create spaces that touch one's soul. There is a blend of peace, simplicity, and grandeur that I have only felt in ancient cathedrals. The harmonics of the space created by the columns and fifty-foot ceilings are not to be found elsewhere. As I walked up a hill to the next community, not a village exactly, but a cluster of houses and a hotel with a playground, I passed a garden center where a man leaped up from his chair behind the heavy gate (everything was fenced in and guarded, even the houses) and came over to the gate to greet me.

"Well?" he repeated several times with great enthusiasm.

I didn't understand what he wanted. This encounter turned out to be one of the many misunderstandings I would experience along the way. He spoke the word "well" as a question in exactly the way an English speaker would when demanding a response to a question, for example:

"Well, what is the answer?

Finally I realized that he was asking:

"Are you well?"

However, something subtle in the inflection and mannerism was off just enough to completely confuse me. After assuring him that I was, in fact, "well," or, as well as could be expected under the circumstances, I continued

Lavender field.

to walk through the small community, past the tour busses parked outside the hotel and out the other end towards Los Arcos. A short time later I came around a curve in the path to a field of lavender in full bloom. The sight was breathtaking. I lingered for a moment amazed and listened to the millions of bees working the flowers. So many bees made quite a loud chorus and I hoped that I wouldn't do anything to annoy one by accident since the consequences could be dire. A paranoid response to nature's bounty, but what can you expect from a person born and raised in New York City? At 1:00 I came to Azqueta, a village with a fine church to St. Peter. As I was having cheese and Irache wine in the tiny garden, the man who keeps the key came out to open the church and show me the inside which was resplendent with

Azqueta Garden.

an awesome 16th century high altar and statues. Quite inspiring. The view across the valley to the Castillo de Deyo is delightful, but I am getting a little concerned about the upcoming terrain, since the key keeper, who has been joined by two of his comrades, informs me that the road ahead is quite steep. I decided to leave my vest here, since it is a beautiful and hospitable village. This is a vest I have treasured for years, but I could think of no better place than Azqueta to let it go and lighten my burden.

Just before entering Villamayor de Monjardín, I lingered briefly at the 13th century Fountain of the Moors. Maybe it was the recent restoration, or just my desire to move on, but the place didn't interest me very much

Fuentede los Moros.

despite its antiquity. In sharp contrast to the hospitality of Azqueta, in the next village, Villamayor de Monjardín, as I admired the church and took a photograph, a hostile man came out to protect and conceal his church from me rather than share its beauty.

It is 3:30 and I begin what seems an interminable march across a forbidding landscape. As fate and poor planning would have it, I begin this March ill-equipped, with neither enough food nor water. There is nothing from here to Los Arcos 12 km away and, while it isn't far, conditions combine to make it arduous. At this hour the sun is high and hot. Everything with any sense is resting in the shade. It is one of those intensely bright afternoons where not even a bug is crawling or bird flying. One feels unusually alone and vulnerable. As I walk the dirt path through fields of wheat, which are mercifully mostly flat, I begin to tire and rest after an hour to drink my last (hot) can of orange-aid, since I am out of water. As I walk again, out of nowhere an old man begins to catch up with me and then disappears suddenly like a phantom. At 5:00 two Frenchmen catch up to me and tell me they left Estella at 2:00. They set a very fast pace which I can't even think of matching and a few minutes later at the top of a rise from where I can see for miles,

Parish Church.

with the road in plain view, the Frenchmen are nowhere to be seen. Like the old man, they have vanished—spooky. After what seems an eternity, I reach Los Arcos and the Refugio that is quite nice. It is a single story contemporary building, clean and uninspiring. After paying my 400 Pts. and selecting my bunk, I make my way to the local grocery store and buy the usual cheese, fruit, and wine and head back to the Refugio to eat. There were several other pilgrims at the kitchen table eating, and what seems like a pleasant discussion (in French) suddenly turns into a heated argument with shouting and gesturing. One of the participants was the Frenchman I met back in Zubiri, otherwise known as "the French guy," who I met later that evening in town as he was checking the bus schedules in an attempt to avoid any further contact with the members of the opposition. He remains a very excitable pilgrim, and while I understood little of what he was saying, it was clear that he was still upset by the altercation back at the Refugio. Each time I came in contact with him, he was bitterly upset by something or someone. Back in Zubiri, it was his guidebook's mistake about the local restaurants being open that had him fuming. After eating, I attended a special pilgrim's Mass at the cathedral, which gave me a chance to explore the square a bit and make a phone call home.

Leaving Villamayor de Monjardin.

June 25

Los Arcos–Viana

Church of the Holy Sepulchres.

Walked out of Los Arcos early, as usual, heading for Viana only 18.5 km away. At 10:30, I arrive at Torres del Río where I have orange juice at the beautiful little 12th century Church of the Holy Sepulchre. This is a very unusual octagonal Romanesque church which some believe to have been built by the Knights Templar, principally because of its resemblance to the octagonal Church of the Holy Sepulchre in Jerusalem that was under their protection. Unfortunately, the church was closed and as I lingered for a moment the group of American students I met back in Estella came through. One guy was carrying two heavy packs. One on front and one in the usual back position. I was told that one of the women had injured her knee and he was helping her out. I was very impressed, not only with his charity but also with his strength. I march onward into a blazing hot sun across a stretch of wheat fields, where the only shelter I found from the sun was a shepherd's stone hut. I ate my last melted chocolate bar from home and put more sun block on my arms, which were not looking good due to overexposure.

Shepherds hut.

According to Aymery de Picaud, a French priest credited with writing a travel guide in 1130, more than half a million people a year made the pilgrimage. Even more make the difficult trip today during holy years, and I console myself that what I am experiencing is not nearly as difficult and treacherous as it was eight centuries earlier. Then, the rivers were polluted, food difficult to obtain and robbers would be a constant threat to your life.

Church of San Pedro.

I reach Viana in an exhausted condition at around 2:00. Although it is early, I decide to stay here at the Refugio, which is one of the finest with only four pilgrims other than myself. A Spanish bicyclist, a German man on two crutches whom I have encountered before, and a Dutch couple, also on bicycles. The Refugio is opposite the 14th century ruins of the church of San Pedro. Since I have my choice of bunks, I select one next to a window overlooking the valley towards Logroño. Below my window there is a public park bordered by a wall beyond which there is a steep drop to the street below. I felt very grateful for the rest here. After a dinner of prosciutto, cheese, bread, tomato, and wine, I watched the sun set at about 9:45. Earlier, I bought a length of rope and some clothespins to hang my laundry on the window casings and after having coffee with the Dutch couple, both of whom are counselors, I turn in. Almost everyone I met from Holland has been a counselor of some sort. I'm not sure if that means that the Dutch are extremely well-balanced from all the care, or in such poor condition that they require lots of therapy. My small sample of encounters is no indication of course, and the people I have met from Holland have been exceptionally warm and well-adjusted people.

Refugio at Viana.

June 26
Viana–Navarrete

Logroño:Fuente de los Peregrinos.

It is 10:30 A.M. and I am having breakfast in the Plaza del Mercado in Logroño after walking the 8.5 km from Viana. This is a beautiful city with its Plaza dominated by a very impressive Cathedral. I spend a little time walking around looking for a store that sells camping supplies with no success. I am trying to buy a lighter sleeping bag than the one I am carrying—something that is just a couple of sheets sewn together. After asking a few people and investigating one or two stores I give up and walk on. This is a city rich in history and well preserved architecture, but at this point, I am too tired and sore to really focus my attention on that aspect of my. Leaving Logroño is an even uglier experience than entering, which was not pretty. Miles of a grim industrial sector and garbage dumps guard the beauty of the city's interior. At about 4:00, thankful to be well free of the smelly industrial wasteland, I stop for lunch at an artificial lake about half way to Navarrete. This is a serene spot with a landscaped park and benches.

At 6:30 after arriving in Navarrete, I take a room at what appears to be the only place in town, the Fonda La Carioca. There is a Refugio under construction (a splendid, comfortable refuge according to my guide), but not yet ready. At the hotel, the proprietor sits at a table near the kitchen working on his books while his wife feverishly scurries around the kitchen preparing dinner. Rather than check me in himself, the woman must interrupt her work and attend to me. I wanted a room with a bath and this took some doing due to our mutual language barrier. Eventually, after consulting with the proprietor three times about prices, and each time the price was reduced, we agreed upon 3,000 Pts. for a room with bath and meals on the third floor. Very expensive and clearly taking advantage of being the only choice in town. The room was adequate, clean and spare with a single bed, side table, chair, and a window overlooking the street. After washing up and resting, I made my way to the dining room back down on the first floor. It is a large room illuminated by a zillion watts of fluorescent light. Dinner is decent but not inspiring consisting of salad, four paper-thin pork chops, french-fries, and melon. There are ten other dinners and the waiter is very efficient, serving meals quickly, and removing the used dishes and utensils almost before the guests have left the table. After dinner I went next door for a café solo. Thank God it was only next-door since my feet were very painful. After coffee I had planned to walk to the church but my feet wouldn't allow it. Instead I returned to my room and lanced a few blisters with a needle, thread, and alcohol wipes.

As I prepare to sleep, I am feeling intensely lonely for the first time. After 8 days of walking, taking meals mostly alone, and no real conversation, it is beginning to get to me. My pilgrimage is undoubtedly the most difficult physical experience of my life (so far). My body is sore, my feet ache, and I have gone out of phase with the few people I was traveling with a few days earlier. Not that we had formed any real friendships, but it was nice to see some familiar faces now and then and say hello.

June 27
Navarrete–Nájera

Breakfast of café con lèche and a roll at 8:30 then back to El Camino that turns out to be about 5 km of road hell.

Highway Hell.

At 3:00 I reached the Refugio at Nájera where I checked in and made myself some lunch of bread and cheese. This is a beautiful Refugio run by Dave, a volunteer from California . We talked a bit, and he offered to help me reorganize my pack with the goal of reducing its weight, which has been a constant annoyance to me. Sitting on my bunk we took everything out of the pack and accessed its value to weight ratio. With Dave's help, I made two piles: the essential and the unnecessary, the latter weighing at least a kilogram (2.2 lbs.), and while seemingly insignificant, it constituted a much welcome reduction in the overall weight of my pack. When I asked Dave when my feet would stop hurting his pithy reply was simply,

"when you stop walking."

I guess I was hoping for a response such as:

"after you go 200 km you will be used to it and everything will be fine."

After rearranging my pack I visited the celebrated church of

Dave from California.

Santa María la Real. Legend holds that in 1052, Don García, the king of Nájera, was hunting when his falcon disappeared into a cave after a dove. When the king went in after them he discovered a statue of the Virgin Mary with Madonna lilies at her feet, and lit by a lamp. The elements of the legend, the statue of the Virgin Mary, the lamp and the Madonna lilies are part of the current church built into the rocks. In addition to the Madonna, the church contains a beautiful Pantheon of the tombs of the Kings of Navarra. I spent an hour or so experiencing the church and the cloisters, which were very inspiring before returning to the Refugio.

Pilgrims relaxing in refugio at Nájera.

At about 8:30 with the town just waking up, I went for a walk down by the River Nájerilla that runs through the town and has parks on both sides. As I sit absorbing the activity of the people playing with their kids and buying food from cart vendors, I try to get a sense of how all these relics relate to contemporary life. I feel as though I am walking through shadows of the past. Even though the past is no longer with us, its presence is so strong on El Camino that it exerts a tangible pull on my consciousness. With the existence of so many fine artistic and architectural masterpieces, the past is every bit as real as the present. While the past may be gone forever, in this place its shadow is long indeed, and I can see it in the buildings and sense it in the people who inhabit the ancient cities and towns. These are the ancestors of those who lived the legends, and through their veins run the blood of the heroes and villains. Yet, like all shadows, there is hollowness. Contemporary Spaniards are not living in the glorious period of their culture represented by the relics of the past surrounding them. The belief systems that inspired the artifacts we admire are no longer in place and as a consequence there are

Cloisters of Santa María la Real.

few, if any, masterpieces being created that could rival the achievements of the glory days. Today's Spaniards are caretakers of an inherited cultural myth that seems to have more of a presence than life in the present. I have had a similar experience traveling in the southwest of the United States. There, the presence of the past is equally powerful, exuding as it does from every adobe hut, and it seems as though the present is overshadowed by the past and lived vicariously through it. Still, I am a willing player in the game of perpetuating the reality of a past epoch. With one leg in the here and now, and the other in the long shadow of history, I trudge along a path worn deep by the sacrifices of countless pilgrims for over a thousand years.

June 28

Nájera–Santo domingo de la Calzada

Magical spot to rest on El Camino.

8:30 A.M.—awoke feeling the flow of the Universe. It rained lightly as I walked up a hill and left Nájera. The rain increased making the trail muddy and hard to negotiate. I reached Azofra at 10:00 wet and soggy and arrived in Santo Domingo De La Calzada around 3:00 after walking 20 km from Nájera. Though I haven't gone very far today, this has been the 11th day of walking and I'm wearing down. I checked into the Refugio, tired, wet, and with aching feet. Very ugly views and smells greet the pilgrim entering the city. The Refugio is on the third floor of an ancient building next to the cathedral and is very clean and comfortable. After having a café solo in an otherwise empty bar I visited the Cathedral famous for having a chicken coop in the church itself. The chickens are there because of a legend that goes like this (from my guidebook):

> "In the 14th century, a man and his wife from Saintes, a part of the diocese of Cologne were making the pilgrimage to Santiago de Compostela, accompanied by their son Hugonell. They stopped for the night at the inn in Santo Domingo, where the innkeeper's daughter took a fancy to the young man, who virtuously resisted her advances. Thus spurned, she hid a silver goblet in Hugonell's baggage, and the following morning denounced him as a thief. The boy was arrested and hanged. As his parents were preparing to depart they heard their son's voice telling them that he was still alive, as St. Dominic was holding him up by the feet. They hastened to the house of the judge, who was just sitting down to dine on a pair of roast chickens, a cock and a hen, and told him the extraordinary tale. The judge retorted that the boy was no more alive than the cock and hen on his plate. At that, the birds jumped out of the plate, grew feathers again and began to flutter around and cackle and crow, thus demonstrating

the hanged boy's innocence."

The Cathedral is very beautiful and there was a mass in progress when I visited. I was impressed with a particularly vivid and tortured statue of the Virgin dressed in black and with arrows piercing her. I can't recall seeing any image of her quite so believable and moving. The chickens were oblivious to both the statue and the mass. After returning to the Refugio, I decided to make some spaghetti with asparagus soup as a sauce for dinner. The kitchen was a bustling place with all of us waiting our turn at the small stove. There was a French couple cooking up a storm who generously shared some of the delicious crepes they made with me.

June 29

Santo Domingo De La Calzada–Belorado

Common area of Belorado refugio.

Belorado 5:30 P.M.—still raining. I washed some clothes in the bathroom, which I'm sure will not be dry by the time I leave in the morning but they needed to be washed anyway. I've had a shower but feel cold and wet. I have been in the Church of Santa Maria next door where I lit a couple of electric candles for my family. Not quite as authentic as the real thing, but better than nothing. The Refugio is clean with a large common area and several sleeping rooms upstairs. The only trouble is that it is quite packed with pilgrims. I manage to find a bunk in a small room (3 meters wide and 7 meters long) with 10 bunks. Mostly Czechs and a single bare light bulb hangs from the center of the ceiling. It is smelly, and at 8:00 P.M. some people are sleeping, some talking, and some have yet to arrive. I had another dinner of spaghetti with tomato sauce I found in one of the cupboards. The Refugio is so crowded that people are sleeping on the benches and floor of the common room. A man from Holland came in late after walking 40 km and told us that he will probably go to Burgos tomorrow, a distance of about 50 km. He was appropriately young and enthusiastic, and I had no doubt he would do exactly as he said. I will be quite satisfied with a walk of about 26 km to San Juan de Ortega where the priest serves legendary garlic soup to all pilgrims following the mass. I resolve to bandage the very serious blisters that have developed on my heels before walking tomorrow and go to bed.

Church of Santa María.

June 30
Belorado–San Juan de Ortega

Ruins of San Felices Apse, 10th C.

8:30 A.M. —having coffee in a bar in Belorado square with André, a Frenchman, and his wiry little Spanish friend while I wait for the bank to open so I can exchange a travelers check. We are talking about the healing aspects of El Camino and Andre shows me a snapshot of a group of about eight pilgrims who have all suffered losses of those close to them. André tells me his own story about how he broke up with his girlfriend and lost his job and how El Camino has helped him to put his life back together. This is something like his seventh pilgrimage—the second this year. I learned later after speaking with Evelyn, an Italian living in France who is writing an article for a magazine and interviewing people as she does the pilgrimage herself, that all may not be what it seems with André. Rather than a healing experience, the pilgrimage may have become an artificial crutch for him—a substitute for life since he really can't function in the real world. We went on to discuss one of his favorite and controversial Refugios, the Aroyo de San Bol, which is run by a character named Louis. It is controversial in the sense that some, like André, find it enriching and admire Louis. Others find him suspicious suggesting drug use in a cult-like atmosphere. In any case, Louis is a charismatic individual who dresses in military fatigues and a beret. He is reputed to be a former Israeli fighter pilot and monk who runs this Refugio

Tent City at Villafranca Montes de Oca.

between Burgos and Castrojeriz which I will visit soon. I assured Andre that I would visit Louis, and after parting, I went to the bank, bought some food, and started on my way. The weather has cleared up, and after 12.5 kilometers I stopped for lunch at Villafranca Montes de Oca where there is a tent city for pilgrims. I spoke to the proprietor for a while and learned that it was due to open in a few days. Although it seemed quite comfortable

San Juan de Ortega.

in a military fashion, I was glad I had no intention of stopping there. Villafranca is an ancient settlement boasting a pilgrim's hospital from as early as the 9th century. I climbed a steep hill and found a spot overlooking the Church of Santiago to sit and have lunch. According to reports, this area was always one of the most difficult parts of the pilgrimage due to its steepness and harsh climate, not to mention the bloodthirsty bandits who robbed and murdered pilgrims. Although the road is very steep, the weather this year is unseasonably cool, and the bandits seem to be under control.

At 5:30 after walking 25.5 kilometers, I reach San Juan de Ortega looking forward to the legendary garlic soup that is served to all pilgrims. After registering with the grumpy fellow who stamped my credentials, I proceeded upstairs to the huge dorm area. I saw at least four very large rooms

Anna & Carlton at rest.

and two bathrooms. After staking out my bunk and washing up I went to the monastery church where the priest offered a short ceremony followed by an excruciating long explanation of the famous capital in the church. It was too long for me because I was chilly and shivering the entire time and couldn't understand a word. When he started, he asked for an interpreter from Spanish to French, but I was apparently in the minority as an English speaker, and therefore, left out of the loop. After what seemed like forever, he finished and we went next door to the large monastery building attached to the church for garlic soup. I asked for and received the recipe which was given as follows:

day old bread
olive oil
garlic (chopped)
beef stock
2 eggs (stirred in).

July 1

San Juan de Ortega–Burgos

Awoke at 7:00 A.M. and had coffee with the priest in the kitchen of the monastery, which is another tradition of San Juan de Ortega. We said little since we did not have a language in common, and I thanked him and went outside in the early morning brisk air. I chatted with a man from Holland who was making the pilgrimage along with his wife on bicycles. He was counselor, of course, and we regretted not having the time to sit and talk more and get to know each other. I started off with a group of five or six pilgrims, some I had seen on and off for several days. Eventually, we found our own pace and split up. I found it continually baffling as I walked through town after town, that nothing was open. No store, no bar—no place where I could have breakfast. I didn't find an open store until well after noon. At 5:30 after 23 kilometers, I finally arrived in Burgos. While I was glad to see a large city for a change, I must admit that walking into it was very unpleasant. One is greeted by several kilometers of industrial suburbia with lots of traffic and air pollution. When I finally reached the city proper I was very tired and unhappy to learn that the Refugio was all the way on the opposite side of the city—another walk of about five kilometers. When I finally reached it I was glad to find that there was a bed available. The Refugio was not the best, nor the worst, I had seen so far. It looked like a summer camp since it was constructed in a park of several single story cabin-like buildings.

Albergue del Peregrino

July 2–3

Burgos–Homillos del Camino

Last night I had coffee in a bar across the river from the Refugio which is also a hostel: Gran Bar Punta Brava for 2,000 Pts. I haven't eaten a decent meal since lunch yesterday where I had eggs in a little town called Orbaneja served by a clumsy waitress. Planning to stay in Burgos another night, this morning I went back to the bar and left my pack with the woman running the bar who said her son handles the hostel and I would have to return later

Cathedral Archway.

to check in. I walked a few kilometers along the river to the center of Burgos and spent several hours checking out the amazing cathedral. I took many photographs and met the Danes who are also spending an extra day here before busing on to the coast. I returned to the hostel, checked in, and went upstairs to wash my clothes and myself. It was a nice feeling to be in a large city for a change, with its crowds and multitude of bars and shops. At about 6:00 P.M. I went downstairs to inquire about dinner and was informed that the appropriate time to eat was 9:00 P.M. Of course! What was I thinking? I returned to my room for a bit of bread and cheese I had left over and decided to head back to town in search of postage stamps, a jacket or sweater since I was still cold, and eat dinner when the restaurants finally open.

Archway detail.

On the way I noticed a crowd of people going into an ancient church and followed them inside to find a magnificent cathedral with an amazing alter. A mass in progress is officiated by an old hunchback priest who unlocks a silver door at the center alter and brings out a chalice with "bread." As he gives communion to the faithful I noticed a wonderful statue of a missionary priest with his hand over his heart. There is a native kneeling at his feet

Larger than life puppets.

and they are both in a state of spiritual bliss with the priest definitely in control. While I have great respect for all religions, this mass brought out all sorts of issues I have with ritual and orthodox religious ceremony. While the ritual is glorious, what it represents in terms of a personal commitment and adherence to doctrine is a bit over the top for a Protestant like myself. Now another priest takes over and speaks at a rapid fire pace as the congregation responds. Afterwards I went into a basement shop a few doors from

Festival dancers.

the church where a man was making botas. I enjoyed the idea of buying one directly from the craftsman who makes them and bought a small .25 liter one (weight is a factor) for 800 pts. Still feeling chilly, I walked another block to a clothes store and bought a very conservative cardigan sweater before proceeded to the HiFi Café for café solo. I enjoyed my café and noticed how urbane, well dressed, and generally civilized the citizens of Burgos are. After leaving the café, I walked across the river to the Plaza Mayor where the spectacle was unbelievable. This being festival week, the crush of people was unlike anything I had ever experienced. Literally thousands of people were crowded into the plaza and I was concerned for the children and old people. Except for me, everyone seemed to take it in stride. Frightening and fun. Live television was there with satellite uplink ready to report every moment of the planned event which was unfolding on a stage I couldn't see. The atmosphere was definitely festive with live music in every corner, including an acid rock band in the shadow of the cathedral.

Burgos shop

Definitely an interesting yet somehow appropriate combination. Peruvian indians, blacks, and Asians were all hawking cool stuff on the street. Bands marching and singing paraded through the narrow streets. I stood in an archway of the cathedral and listened to an exceptional band and watched the revelers. Old, young, and teenagers, danced and drank with total abandon. These people know how to party! The bars are absolutely packed with revelers spilling out into the street. Eventually, I find a small restaurant and enjoy the best dinner of roast lamb and melon desert I've had in Spain. The next morning I leave late after yet another comical experience exchanging American Express Travelers checks. My advice is to never use them and stick to credit card cash advances—much easier and convenient. After entering the bank and handing the teller my check, two men begin working on the project of cashing it. While one is holding it up to the light, turning it over and over and examining it closely, the other is making phone calls about it. Suddenly, the machine spits out a receipt and I have the cash. The transition from appearing to have never seen a travelers' check before to business as usual was very amusing.

French pilgrim, Wanni, and Evelyne compare notes.

At 2:15 P.M. I was having lunch in Rabé de Las Calzadas. Local kids are practicing disco in the streets to Saturday Night Fever and other than the dancers there isn't a soul in sight. As I am enjoying my lunch a woman traveling alone passes by. I feel tired and my pack seems unusually heavy. Too much resting in Burgos, I suppose, has made me lazy.

July 4
Hornillos del Camino–Castrojeriz

After spending the night in Hornillos del Camino, which has a pleasant and modern Refugio, I continued to Aroyo de san Bol where I looked forward to meeting the legendary Louis. I walked part of the 11 kilometers with Evelyn and Wanni her friend from the Canary Islands. The weather is perfect and as we walked we encountered an American cyclist and a French pilgrim, traveling individually in the opposite direction from us. They had already been to Santiago and were on their way back to where they started.

Inside Aroyo de san Bol (Pepe & Louis 3rd & 4th from left).

I was very impressed with the French pilgrim who had a notable sense of serenity about her. Also I didn't meet very many pilgrims who returned to their homes on foot, as did the pilgrims of old.

Aroyo de san Bol is a single building a few kilometers off the main track.

A relaxing lunch at Aroyo de san Bol.

When I arrived Louis and the group of pilgrims sitting inside talking and eating warmly welcomed me. At first I thought that a man called Pepe was Louis since he was loud, had a commanding presence and dominated the group. But, as it turned out, Louis was the quieter smaller fellow wearing a beret. He was a very attentive host and after we talked for awhile, he set about to prepare a lunch for us of bread and soup with the help of an assistant. More pilgrims drifted in, and as we sat down to lunch there were about 10 of us. I had an interesting conversation with one of his regular guests about the fate of the Knights Templar. There was another rumor about Louis being a member of a contemporary Templar secret society. We ate lunch outside the building in a pleasant courtyard and were amused by Louis who picked up a pair of powerful binoculars to examine all new pilgrims traveling the main road across a field. We ate and talked for awhile before getting our things together and heading out towards Castrojeriz about 16 km ahead.

I must say that I noticed no unusual or uncomfortable vibes at Aroyo de san Bol or in the person of Louis. I walked the last part of the way to Castrojeriz with Wanni discussing our respective lives and plans. As we approached

Louis & Evelyne.

the town down a long straight road lined with poplar trees, it struck me as being one of the most beautiful towns I had seen so far. It is situated around a large high hill with a ruined castle dominating the very top—very medieval in feeling. On the way to the Refugio we visited a beautiful church that was a perfect introduction to Castrojeriz. We wove our way through the streets to the Refugio and upon entering were handed a song sheet and joined in singing pilgrim songs with great enthusiasm for about half an hour. The same charismatic old pilgrim who dominated the gathering at Aroyo de san Bol led the singing. Afterwards I made my way upstairs to claim a bunk and wash up a bit before finding my dinner in a local bar with a young German named Gerhardt.

July 5
Castrojeriz–Frómista

Long shadows leaving Castrojeriz.

The next morning I awoke to liturgical chants and one of the hosts walking through the dorm gently but firmly encouraging people to be up and ready. They served us coffee and cookies and had us on our way by 8:00 A.M. as usual. This was one of the most comfortable Refugios located in a building with a garden and courtyard in the old section of town. Leaving Castrojeriz was even more spectacular than arriving. The morning was crisp and bright with that unique quality of Spanish morning sun that seems to illuminate everything from within and throw mysteriously long shadows. After walking down the hill that the town is situated on and across a flat plain for a few kilometers, the road rose steeply to the top of a plateau called Mostelares. I walked alone to that point, passed by only one pilgrim who was muttering and chanting to himself. As I crested the top of the plateau I encountered a large cross and a group of pilgrims singing the same pilgrim songs with gusto, led by none other than Pepe, the same guy who led the singing back at the Refugio. I must say that I admired his spirit even if it did seem a bit fanatical.

Castrojeriz in the distance.

I really enjoyed this bit of geographic oddness since it was rare and a beautiful experience. Looking back, which was always one of my favorite things to do, was especially rewarding from the top of the plateau. Resting from the very steep climb up to the top of the plateau, I could see Castrojeriz far in the distance. This is the type of experience that I never have had before, neither at home nor anywhere else—to stand at the top of a mountain looking back and know that as far as the eye can see, I have walked it. Castrojeriz looked charming perched on its own little hill in the midst of a great plain. It was easy to see why they built a castle at the top. After a bit I stopped at Fuente de Piojo, a fountain, and rested.

San Nicholas.

There was a small park with benches and tables built around the fountain, and it was here that I first met Bill, an Art Education teacher from Milwaukee, and Aitor, his Basque friend. At this point my feet and legs were suffering from wearing a pair of cheap sandals that I bought in an attempt to relieve the serious blisters on both my heals. We walked as a group eventually coming to a fine little church, the San Nicholás, where everyone stopped and rested while admiring the small chapel. This restored church had very strong positive energy and was quite a rewarding experience. After a few more kilometers I stopped at a bar to rest and write. I had two café solos listening to very loud music while a television silently showed us the news. As I was leaving the bar I ran into Gerhardt, a German farmer, with whom I walked to Boadilla del Camino, a pleasant little town where we had lunch at about 3:00. After lunch we walked very quickly, covering the 5 km to Frómista in about an hour.

Interior of San Nicholas.

The walk was hot and followed a man-made canal. After crossing the lock we entered Frómista, which, although rich with history, seemed to have little beyond the monuments to recommend it. The town was flat and low, and looked as though it had just sprouted a few days before. The Church of San Martin is a remarkable jewel but so highly and immaculately restored that it seemed to me to have lost its charm. I am once again impressed with the absence of any graffiti on these buildings. Granted they are national treasures, but in the U.S. I'm sure they would be targets despite their antiquity. The penalty for defacing them must be no less than hanging. The Refugio was crowded and uninteresting, and after a little sightseeing, dinner of cheese and bread from the local shop with Gerhardt, I resolved to pack it in and leave at sunrise in order to get out of Frómista as soon as possible.

July 6
Frómista– Carrión de los Condes

San Zoilo.

As planned, I left Frómista at 5:30 A.M. while it was still dark. It was good starting early before everyone was up and about and miss the crowds. 22 km later at 10:00 I had my credentials stamped at the convent of Santa Clara in Carrión de los Condes where St. Francis of Assisi was thought to have been given shelter. In order to get stamped, a nun came to a deep window with bars on both sides and a rotating shelf onto which the credential to be stamped was placed and passed to a nun on the other side. The arrangement was designed to avoid any contact between the sisters and lay people who came to visit. At the other end of town I spent some time in the beautiful San

Zoilo monastery which is also a luxury hotel or parador. The cloisters, tombs of the princes, and elegant carvings on the capitals were very moving and I appreciated the rest after a long morning's walk.

Last night I dreamed that people were telling me that I had done this incredible thing for which I received a certificate. The dream obviously referred to the pilgrimage, but another aspect of the dream was that I was very surprised by the news of what I had done since I had no memory of it. It was as though I was asleep during the entire pilgrimage and awoke to the news of having done something notable. I took this to be a wake-up call. Was I asleep at that very moment? Would I walk the entire Camino in a trance? I thought about this and made a special effort to awaken as I considered the skulls beautifully carved into the columns of Zoilo's cloisters—there to remind us that time is short.

Now I entered what I like to think of as the "badlands" since this stretch of the Camino was particularly difficult for me. Right up there with the two or three hardest parts of the journey, such as the second day crossing the Pyrenees when I thought I would die. It probably has more to do with my condition at that particular time rather than anything unusually challenging about the road. Nevertheless, soon after leaving San Zoilo the way became part of an ancient Roman road that was characteristically straight as well as rocky. I was wearing sneakers in order to allow the blisters to heal and had my hiking boots strapped to my pack making it feel even heavier. This road, while only about 17 km, seemed endless. It was very hot with the brutal Spanish sun directly overhead and my feet and legs hurt from the 22 km I already walked in the morning. I have been walking for 17 days and I am in no better condition than when I started—significantly worse, in fact.

Roman ordeal.

But this road was especially deceptive. An added difficulty was that I had misjudged my water supply and had to ration it carefully to avoid running out since there was nothing between Carrión de los Condes and Calzadilla de la Cueza. And that emptiness was part of the psychological difficulty of this stretch of road—the dreary, boring, nearly flat lonely quality of it. No villages, or even buildings, just fields of cereal as far as the eye could see. I had to keep to the sides of the road as much as possible since the sneakers I was wearing were no match for the rocks and the souls of my feet hurt with every step. The road began to play insidious tricks on me—as I walked towards the horizon it would suddenly and continually grow further away as I crested an almost unnoticeable upward grade. This trickery of never seeming to make progress continued for four hours until I really though I had reached the limit of my endurance. Then like a miracle, as I crested yet another slight rise, the town of Calzadilla de la Cueza lay before me only 100 meters away. It was completely invisible before that moment and the feelings of relief and gratitude were overwhelming.

Resting pilgrims.

Thankfully, the Refugio was on this end of town and I was given water from a jug immediately upon entering. It was quite full with pilgrims who had arrived before me, some getting checked in and finding their beds, while others sat in the backyard, talking and tending their blisters. This Refugio was a simple house in a row of houses in the town, with a second floor containing several rooms where pilgrims slept. After my credentials were stamped, the hostess offered to help me by carrying my pack upstairs (I must have looked a wreck) but when the young woman bent down to pick it up, she couldn't lift it off the floor As I lifted the pack she scolded me for carrying such a heavy load and I resolved again to lighten my load as soon as possible. There were no beds or bunks upstairs, just mattresses on the floor packed in as tightly as possible. This was not an appealing sight. I knew that my loud snoring would bother the other pilgrims and begged her to allow me to sleep downstairs somewhere. She didn't think there really was anyplace but finally decided to let me put a mattress on the floor in a downstairs hallway which was a great relief for my sudden and severe case claustrophobia. They were turning away pilgrims now, so I just made it in at the last minute. Then the bed people showed up. This was one of the most unusual encounters of the pilgrimage. A German couple was transporting an actual bed on a cart by pushing and pulling it with bicycles. They had started in Germany and were well on their way to completing their mission of reaching Santiago de Compostela.

Bed People.

The arrival of the "bed people" caused quite a stir among the pilgrims, and of course everyone was curious about their motivation. As it turns out, despite some discussion and distribution of literature by the bed people, it seemed that no one fully understood their motive, including me. Briefly, it seems that the bed was a relic from a holocaust site and their transporting it to Santiago was in some way a national penitence, though that aspect was downplayed in favor of the pilgrimage being a performance or art piece of sorts. I believe they also had personal motives. In any case, we all marveled at their commitment and were amused to see that they installed the bed in the backyard and actually slept on it as though it were a camper. A couple of Frenchmen also decided to forego the crowded second floor quarters and camped out in their sleeping bags outside in the backyard. This too was the source of quite a bit of joking and teasing especially since they turned in quite early in the evening. Eventually, at about 8:30, after eating some remnants of food I had brought with me, and everyone finished their toilet duties, things settled down and I was able to place my mattress and end a very long and excruciating day of walking 40 km in extreme conditions.

July 7
Carrión de los Condes–Sahagún

Church of La Trinidad.

I arrived in Sahagún at about noon. Although the walk was only 15 km, yesterday's ordeal wore me down and made today's walk difficult despite the short distance. I walked part of the way on the highway because the rocks hurt the bottoms of my feet so bad and got lost a couple of times since I was off the marked Camino. By the time I got to Sahagún I felt like a cripple: my feet and legs hurt, along with what seemed like every bone in my body. As I walked, I tried to get into a "Zen" thing, that is, acknowledging and being with the pain. Didn't work. What did revive me was checking into the Refugio at the Church of La Trinidad that resembled a warehouse from the outside. Once inside, however, I experienced the splendor of what is probably the most sumptuous Refugio on el Camino. Recently restored, it seemed like a luxury hotel with modern showers and kitchen facilities.

After a shower and nap, I was beginning to feel halfway human again and went out to explore the city. Sahagún has a rich history, and at one point was

Sleeping quarters of la Trinidad refugio.

one of the most influential and powerful monasteries on the road to Santiago. Alfonso VI founded the monastery in the 9th century and the village in 1085. A fire destroyed most of Sahagún in the 19th century and I enjoyed photographing some of the ancient ruins. At this point in my pilgrimage, I was working on a series of photographs called "Sacred Corners" which consists pictures of obscure and often unnoticed corners of the villages and cathedrals I encountered. The series is based on my perception that often there is a focused spiritual energy in the quietly ignored corners of some buildings in addition to the obvious points of power such as the alter. I was glad to hook up with Bill and Aitor around 7:15 for wine and cheese, and we decided to have dinner together along with the Basque family (a couple and their daughter). We found a comfortable little restaurant and ordered garlic soup, trout, wine, and flan—all for 1,000 Pts.

Church of San Tirso, Sahagún.

This was a great treat for me since I had survived mostly on food I buy in the local shops and only rarely sit down to a meal in a restaurant. At dinner we discussed motives for the pilgrimage with Bill being the most forthcoming and explaining that he wanted to follow a tradition begun by his ancestors who migrated west from Chicago. We stopped for coffee at a little place near the Refugio to end a perfectly pleasant and relaxing evening. That night I had a dream that was very simple but felt like a revelation: the strict present is the key. The secret is that everything seems to happen in the past or the future and we never see the present.

Sacred Corner, Church of San Tirso, Sahagún.

July 8

Sahagún–El Burgo Raneros

After Sahagún.

Wallking out of Sahagún on a highway where large trucks almost blew me over was not pleasant. I stopped at one point to ask directions from an old toothless gentleman who was holding a dead mouse. Quite a character. After his careful instructions we parted and soon after several cyclists who had also stayed at La Trinidad stopped me. One of them held up my mini Mag-light, a small and invaluable flashlight that I had apparently left behind at the Refugio. I thanked them profusely and earnestly, since I had come to rely on it a great deal. At about 11:00 I arrived at the church of Iglesia del Salvador at Bercianos and went in to experience the Mass that was under way. As is often the case, the Mass is attended only by a handful of old folk and some children. The church was beautiful, simple, and serene. After the

Mass I ate some lunch on a bench next to the church before continuing. At this point the way is transformed into a contemporary straight and tree-lined road that stretches 32 km to Mansilla de las Mulas. This is a lovely idea but it makes for a very dull and uneventful walk. The monotony of the walk is emphasized by the flat terrain and the absolute regularity of the trees, which are all young, straight and equally spaced. These trees are irrigated by an ingenious underground system of hoses that come to life every so often to water them. After a very hot and boring walk I reached El Burgo Raneros at about 1:30 P.M. This small village seemed a bit desolate, though I must admit that I didn't explore it beyond the area of the Refugio, which is near where I entered the village. My guidebook's glowing description of the refuge as "one of the most elegant and authentic" seemed a bit overstated to me. While it was quite new and comfortable, with bunk beds in several rooms upstairs, it seemed a little less grand than the guidebook's description. No doubt I was spoiled by the truly spectacular facilities at Sahagún, and anything short of a five star resort would pale in comparison. After settling in and doing my wash, I walked across the street to the local bar restaurant which was quite lively with locals and pilgrims. I sat at a table and had beer and a few snacks of boiled eggs and other tapas. Meanwhile Gerhardt, the German pilgrim enters and orders dinner that he will take in the adjoining dinning room. This idea appeals to me so I join him in ordering salad and calamari that we eat while discussing the relatively boring tree lined path we have been walking lately. I departed at 6:00 the following morning and continued along the tree lined walkway to Mansilla de las Mulas where I arrived at 10:30 A.M. glad to have finished with the "modern Camino."

July 9
El Burgo Raneros– Mansilla de Las Mulas

Although I had to wait to register at the Refugio in Mansilla de LasMulas while the staff cleaned up after last night's pilgrims, I could tell just by standing in the front room that this was a well organized Refugio. My guidebook tells me that this is one of the most spacious and best-equipped hostels to be found on the pilgrim's route and it is certainly true. In fact, this Refugio is

Courtyard, Mansilla refugio

almost legendary in that it has a washing machine for clothes, a rare amenity that I have been hearing about for days from other pilgrims. .

I went across the street to a bar to have coffee and a snack while I waited, and Pepe, the old pilgrim who led the singing at Castrojeriz was there loudly carrying on as usual. The bar was not very full at 10:30 in the morning and I enjoyed waiting. When I returned to the Refugio they still weren't ready, but several other pilgrims were there and they finally just gave in and allowed us to enter and claim our bunks. The hosts insisted on operating the washing machine, which was in heavy demand, and I put my clothes in the queue to be washed despite the fact that it was raining on and off and seemed unlikely that they would dry before morning. Still, it is so rare to have the opportunity to have my laundry done, I couldn't resist. Meanwhile, I walked around village a bit with Bill, the American professor, and looked at the wall and two locked churches. Mansilla de las Mulas is well know for its walls which were built at the end of the 12th century, one stretch being more or less in tact. Bill and I discussed the idea of walking through León, which is only 13 km further and going to Villadangos, which would add another 20.5 km. It continued to drizzle on and off as I sat in the courtyard listening to liturgical chants and talking to Alexandro whom I had first met in Frómista. Alexandro is an interesting guy who was traveling with a friend and is a biologist by profession. We talked for a long while, mostly me asking questions about Spain and Alexandro very graciously and carefully answering. He pulled out a map and described the various regions, negative population trends, and aspects of agricultural and manufacturing production. He manages a forest in central Spain near Segovia. At this point in my pilgrimage, the blisters on my Achilles heels were deep and still refusing to heal. How could they when everyday they are subjected to more of the same punishment? Anyway, Bill was having a leg problem and Aitor was kind enough to chaperone us both to the local clinic and act as our interpreter. At first it was a little unsettling since the next door to the clinic was a veterinarian, and I couldn't help wondering if they shared doctors. The service was very quick and organized with a minimum of bureaucratic fuss. We waited to see the doctor in a long hallway, very clean and modern, and not too many people. After about half an hour it was my turn and we all three went into the doctor's office where he looked at my heels. His prescription was to keep it clean and he bandaged it up with thick gauze pads. I really appreciated the attention, but I knew that the thick bandages were never going to work inside my boots. Nevertheless, we thanked him and left. It is a tribute to the Spanish that they take such good care of the thousands of pilgrims who tramp through their country every year. Offering free medical support to any pilgrim is a universally understood and long standing tradition that eases the anxiety of many pilgrims as they face the rigors of el Camino. Aitor, Bill, and I ate dinner together in a fine little restaurant close to the Refugio. I had a noodle soup followed by salmon, both of which were excellent. We discussed the small statue of Santiago we had seen in a church that we happened upon just before eating. I thought that the statue was unusual in that it had a prominent thigh wound which immediately identified it with the story of Percival and the Holy Grail. Upon returning to the Refugio, I checked to see how my clothes were drying, which, of course, was very slowly. I had no doubt that I would be carrying wet clothes tomorrow. As I was settling in I happened to mention my blisters to the Norwegian couple who immediately offered to give me their high tech solution—a new type of bandage called endoderm, or second skin. This is a very thin, self-sticking bandage you apply and simply leave on the wound until it heals. It was very effective and made it much easier for me to walk. Also, it didn't bulk up the way the gauze bandage the doctor gave me did. I was immensely grateful. The Norwegians are a delightful retired couple who seem to spend a fair amount of time traveling and exploring. They are both healthy and positive and we talked for awhile about pilgrimages in Norway. Apparently Norwegians like to hike and there are several trails up into the mountains with shelters provided, but with no religious or other significance. I returned to the courtyard where a bunch of pilgrims were sitting around a table talking, playing guitar, singing, and generally enjoying themselves. These were mostly Spanish pilgrims and as the evening wore on, they decided to hold a special Galician ceremony to ward off evil spirits. It consisted of chanting the "Conjuro vara la Queimada," and drinking a special potion made up of Ozujo (from Galicia), orange and lemon rinds, coffee beans, and sugar. After a few rounds of this potion we were all very sure that we had beaten back the evil and called up the divine. It was getting late, however, and someone yelled out of a window for us to terminate the ceremony. Still, to make sure, we decided to have one more round of chanting and magic potion. Halfway into it the Norwegian came down in his under shorts and roundly chastised us for several minutes, carefully reminding us of the rules (lights out and quiet by 8:00) and that there was a house full of tired pilgrims trying to rest for tomorrow's walk. Well, needless to say, the scolding we got from the Norwegian put a damper on the mood and we broke up and retired. At 6:30 the next morning my head was feeling the full force of the magic potion as I sat down to coffee and biscuits graciously provided by our hosts. At 7:00 I left the land of ritual and as the sun rose I stood on the bridge over the river Esla and took a photograph of the ancient walls.

Esla River.

July 10
Mansilla de Las Mulas–León

León Cathedral.

As I set out from Mansilla de las Mulas at sunrise El Camino paralleled a road for a few kilometers before coming to Villarente. Here I had to ask for directions at one point just before the historic bridge Puente de Villarente and entering the village, which seemed rather ordinary but, I am happy to report, had a bar that was open that also had pastries. Naturally I took advantage of the situation and stopped for café and a pastry. The hosts were very welcoming and the bar was clean and inviting with nice little round tables. I was the only patron. As I continued on, I felt better and I must admit I don't remember very much about this stretch until I came to the top of a hill on a highway overlooking León. This was all highway walking which is very unpleasant. Entering León, like most large cities, is not pretty, with an industrial or commercial section that it is necessary to walk through before entering the city. As I started down the long hill, León proper was still several kilometers in the distance, one of the participants in last night's ritual passed me. We said a polite hola as he passed. This young man had the most unusual and amusing walk I have ever seen. He would be a candidate for Monte Python's Bureau of Funny Walks for sure. The key to his extreme individuality was the way he swung his arms with added little jiggles at the end of each stroke. After several minutes of walking down the long hill past huge and slick corporate headquarters of banks and other wealthy enterprises, I suddenly, and without warning, experienced excruciating pain in my right shin. It was so sudden and intense that I thought something had snapped and I had to stop. Nothing like this had ever happened to me before. Naturally, I was quite concerned—not to mention feeling great pain. After standing still for a minute, I continued very slowly, with each step an ordeal. I had to take very small steps and progress was quite slow. I knew that I would never make Santiago de Compostela in this condition. In fact, I wondered if I would even make it the kilometer or so to where the city proper started. Eventually I was able to make it into the city and I knew that my best hope was to find a bandage for my aching tendon. On the way down the hill I noticed a large mall or shopping center not too far from where I was and I headed for it thinking that there would be a store with first aid supplies. When I reached the store, which was a huge place, I asked for bandages as best I could in my nonexistent Spanish, and finally, once I got the idea across, a manager very graciously escorted me into the private area where they had medical supplies and bandaged up my leg. She gave me some rubbing ointment and aspirin and sent me on my way. I felt a bit better, but still limped like a cripple, which is exactly what I was.

León Cathedral.

Outside the store there were several taxis and I limped over to one and asked him to take me to the cathedral. In my pronunciation of the word "cathedral," I emphasized the second syllable— usual for English speakers.

León Cathedral.

Consequently, all I got from the taxi driver was a blank stare and he drove away with another passenger. I tried a second driver and got the same blank stare. In desperation, I just kept repeating the word cathedral, and luckily, by pure accident, I managed to pronounce it in a way that he understood. He immediately spoke the word properly for Spanish speakers, with the emphasis on the last syllable, and I gratefully repeated it several times as we placed my backpack in the trunk of the taxi and got into the passenger seat grateful for a temporary solution. We drove off and before too long, after winding up and down side streets, arrived at the cathedral.

Seeing the magnificent structure for the first time was breathtaking. It sits in back in the center of a large open square on top of a hill. León Cathedral is commanding. After paying my fair, I hobbled into a bar on the edge of the square and ordered a brandy and café solo. Now I was feeling slightly better and briefly visited the cathedral before going to an adjacent building along the side of the square in search of a stamp for my pilgrim's credentials. At long last, after walking through several long corridors, I came to a room where an official sat behind a desk and cheerfully stamped my pilgrims passport and directed me to the Refugio. The Refugio was apparently many city blocks away, which concerned me considering my condition, but off I went, asking for new directions every so often. Just as I was thinking that I had become terribly lost, I entered a small square lined with bars filled with tourists and pilgrims. As I passed one bar with tables outside, there sat a young woman who I recognized from Mansilla having drinks with a friend. We greeted each other warmly and she introduced me to her friend, Win. Then she directed me to the Refugio which was located in building owned by the Dominicans, adjacent to their monastery, and which was very close-by. Slowly I made my way to it and checked in. This Refugio was actually the courtyard and gymnasium of a school. The gym was a large open space that doubled as a playing court and auditorium, since there was a stage at one end. There were showers and toilet facilities and several large piles of mattresses in one corner.

Ancient Corner, León.

Quite interesting actually, provided you didn't want privacy of any kind. I pulled down a mattress and claimed a corner of the gym as my space before taking a shower and washing my socks. I was told that the doctor was scheduled to visit later at 10:00 P.M. and that all pilgrims were to attend the chanting held in the chapel next door at 7:00. As it is only 13 km from Mansilla de las Mulas, I arrived in León early at about 11:00 A.M., and after settling into the Refugio, I went to have lunch at 3:30. Naturally, I did not want to walk far, so I went back to the busy little square where I ran into the pilgrims from Mansilla. Here I ran into Alexandro, the biologist, and his friend and we ate together at a restaurant at one end of the square. I had a wonderful lunch consisting of a large plate of spaghetti, filet of beef, salad, ice cream, wine and coffee for 1300 pts. We discussed the Basques, bull fighting, and the San Fermin festival (lay down if you fall—don't get up and run since it is better to be trampled by bulls than gored by them). After lunch I returned to the Refugio gymnasium and napped for awhile before other pilgrims woke me. While I sat in the courtyard writing, Elizabeth, a young American girl who taught at the Montessori school in St. Louis introduced herself to me. I had noticed her earlier talking and giggling with her companion who was Spanish. She told me that she was visiting Italy when, on a whim, she decided to travel to Barcelona and while there heard about the pilgrimage and simply decided on the spot to begin. They were traveling at an accelerated pace, up to 50 km a day, and still had plenty of energy. I couldn't help but envy the energy and free spirit she embodied. At 7:00 in the small lavish chapel the incense is lit and about 25 nuns file in and begin their singing and chants. It was a truly fine experience and I tried to allow the music wash over me and relax into it with only moderate success. Afterwards, I went back up the hill to the cathedral and sat at one of the tables of a café where I could see the cathedral and watch the paseo. The cathedral was beautifully lit and the citizens of León were equally impressive as they strolled past, the young and old, entire families, groups of friends—really quite extraordinary and a delightful end to a trying day. Back at the Refugio, I met with the doctor who was very kind and patient. She massaged my leg and gave me bandages and an anti-inflammatory pill, which, didn't seem to help. Because I was injured I would be allowed to stay another night at the Refugio. I really didn't want to even though I liked León quite a bit. I would simply have to wait until tomorrow to find out if I would be able to continue to travel or not.

Sidewalk, León.

July 11
León– Villar de Marzarife

I awoke early as usual and was glad that my leg felt a bit better, though still very tender. Actually it hurt a lot and I wasn't at all sure that I could continue. Nevertheless, I got my gear together and headed up to the cathedral to say my farewells to it and have one last look. I felt a special fondness for it and enjoyed making photographs of some of the exterior details. I was becoming more and more uncertain about going on today because of my leg. Although I could limp around I was in fear of it suddenly going into a spasm as it did yesterday and preventing me from walking. I wouldn't want that to happen out on the Camino in the middle of nowhere. Had an extra café or two before finally deciding to head out. Leaving León was easier said than done since I was off the marked trail and had to thread my way through village. Basically, I just decided to follow a group of pilgrims who looked like they knew where they were going. Just before leaving the area of the cathedral I ran into Win, the Hollander who directed me when I first entered León. We talked for awhile and she said that she was concerned about having no rain gear and was debating about buying some or not. Being a tenderfoot myself, I really couldn't advise her with any authority, but suggested that she needn't stress out too much over it. I told her that I was carrying a simple vinyl parka. I had the feeling she was just as apprehensive as I was about leaving the comfort of a big city. She asked me to pick up a message for her at Hospital de Órbigo, which was about a days walk further on. We parted company, I on my way out of village, and she off to buy a slicker. After gazing at one of Antonio Gaudi's buildings I walked on past the Real Basilica de San Isadore toward the Hostel de San Marcos on the River Bernesga which I had to cross. I must say that my infirmed condition and concern prevented me from appreciating any of these remarkable buildings. Essentially, I was concentrating on putting one foot in front of the other and simply carrying on without getting run over by a car. Avoiding vehicles was no small accomplishment, I might add, especially crossing the Plaza de San Marcos, which was huge and drivers offered no special leniency to crippled pilgrims who were trying to get across and not staying within the proper walkways. I did manage to make it, of course, and felt less and less confident the closer I got to the outskirts of León proper. At noon I limped into Virgen del Camino, 7 km out of León. As I entered the village, fighter jets flew low in their approach to a nearby airfield jarring any pilgrim out of romantic fantasies about walking the ancient road. If that didn't do it, the specter of the Sanctuary of the Virgen del Camino certainly would. Despite the 13 huge bronze statues adorning the front of the building, this specimen of modern architecture is a far cry from any of the ancient cathedrals I encountered so far, and pales in comparison to the Gothic wonder of the cathedral in León. It stands as a shrine to the shepherd Alvar Simon to whom the Virgen appeared and instructed to build a shrine around 1514. I have no idea what became of the original shrine, but the event sparked the spread of the cult of the Virgen del Camino which spread rapidly. I immediately entered what seemed to be the only bar which was across the street from the Shrine. I was the only customer and ordered a café solo from the man behind the counter who had a distinctly sour disposition. Having encountered the full spectrum of bartenders from gracious and hospitable to grumpy pilgrim haters, I drank my café undaunted by his hostility. I looked over the postcards and was considering purchasing one until I noticed the outrageous price in line with the cost of the café solo. At this point something very interesting occurred. After leaving the bar and crossing a highway to get back on el Camino, I came to a place where the paved road, my map, and the pilgrim yellow arrows all indicated going straight, while a sharp left hand turn would take me across a field on an alternate route. Painted on the road were instructions indicating that the way to Villar de Marzarife was to the left. At the Refugio in León I had picked up a little pamphlet giving directions to Villar de Marzarife and had heard rumors of there being an art museum and talented artist living there. So here I was faced with a choice: go straight for the direct traditional shorter route, or turn left for the alternate route and include the museum and artist. Another element thrown into the decision was the fact that I

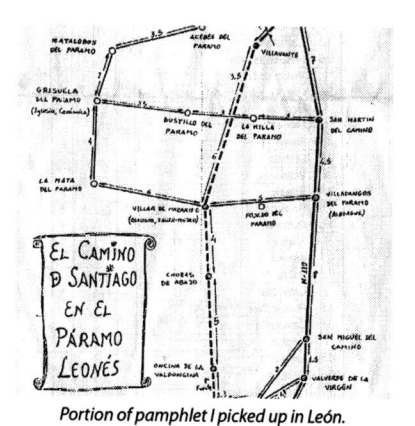

Portion of pamphlet I picked up in León.

was about to embark on a trek across the stark Leónese plain, the prospects of which did not seem appealing. I considered my choice for a moment, checked the status of my right shin, which was throbbing as I stood looking at my map, and walked straight ahead. There was little contest between the two choices actually. My poor condition mandated the straight on path. After walking a short way, the paved road I was on turned slightly left and I continued following the yellow arrows. After about half an hour I came to delightful little village situated in a gully, beautiful old houses and a fountain in the small square. As was not unusual I saw not a single soul stirring. It was another Spanish ghost village of the sort I have become so used to. I stopped to rest on a shady bench by a house and drank a sip of water. Just then I heard someone coming along the road and when I looked up I was surprised to see Win, the woman I had spoken to as I left León. We greeted each other and after splashing a bit of water on our faces at the fountain started off. Even though the temperature was about 82 degrees Fahrenheit, the sun was very hot in a cloudless sky and I put on some sunscreen lotion just before leaving the pleasant little village. As we walked it became evident from our conversation that we were heading for Villar de Mazarife and I indicated my surprise. I told her of my decision to forego the artist and museum and she wondered about my ability to follow instructions that were all over the road. I told her that I saw the signs clearly and deliberately walked straight where she says she turned left. It was disconcerting, but somewhere along the way I must have missed a yellow arrow and taken the wrong path. As we walked, Win told me about herself. Back in Holland she quit her job as a legal secretary and shaved her head just before starting her pilgrimage. She told me that if she concentrated on her heart she could produce ecstatic states and that she worked with a shrink and a Chinese master who was able to produce ecstatic states also, but that she didn't get along with either of them. She talked of having met illuminated people. "How did you know they were illuminated?" I asked. "Because they smiled a lot." Clearly Win wasn't telling me everything. I carefully considered her assessment of pilgrims as a group being "not quite a full shilling" and after applying the test to myself I decided she was correct. At 7:00 we arrived in Villar de Mazarife feeling hot, tired, and dusty. There were signs directing us to the museum that turned out to be a small private house containing the work of the artist who lived there. For some reason I declined a visit down the stairs to this private museum and waited outside while Win entered and had her credentials stamped. Maybe it was the entrance fee that put me off, or the fact that I was here by mistake. I really don't know why I decided to pass on the artist. When she came out we trudged up the road to the Refugio, which was a short distance away. This was a simple yet typical two-story house in a row of houses on the street. Inside there was no kitchen or shower, but it had a lovely courtyard with a balcony on the upper level overlooking it. There were only a few people there including Philip, a Canadian, and his American companion Jennifer who I met up with off and on at various Refugios. After settling in and selecting a bed on the floor upstairs, I walked into the center of village to the Super Spar grocery store and bought cheese, wine and assorted fruit. I stopped at the bakery for bread on the way back and felt prepared for the next day's walk. There were so few people at the Refugio that I actually had a small room to myself. I shared the food and wine I bought with Win, Philip and anyone

Courtyard, Villar de Mazarife.

else who was interested and talked a bit with Philip while Win was off a separate small table in the courtyard writing. After retiring that evening, I woke around midnight to use the lavatory downstairs in the courtyard. Afterwards I stepped out into the middle of the courtyard where I could see the sky and when I looked up I saw the Milky Way for the first time on my pilgrimage. I looked up at the clearly visible and glorious galaxy I thought of the idea that it mirrors el Camino here on earth and of my destination still far to the west.

July 12
Villar de Marzarife–Astorga

Puente de Orbigo.

8:30 A.M. and I am the last to leave the Refugio at Villar de Mazarife. It is a perfect day and after four hours of walking I arrive at Puente de Órbigo and the famous bridge over the river Órbigo. I cross the bridge and after looking down the main street of Hospital de Órbigo, which runs straight through village, I decide to retrace my steps a few meters to the bar situated immediately over the bridge. The bar looks quite fancy and expensive, but I am tired and decided to have a café solo and brandy anyway. The bartender does not seem pleased to see a smelly and dirty pilgrim in his fine establishment, and fortunately, there are no other customers. I take the best seat in the house, a leather couch immediately in front of double glass doors leading out to a patio and with a magnificent view of the bridge. The bridge is famous for an incident in 1434 when a Leónese knight, Don Suero de Quinones, challenged any other knights who wanted to cross the bridge for a

Bar at the end of the bridge.

period of about a month. Don Suero declared that he was imprisoned by his love for a lady and vowed to break 300 lances as ransom to escape his prison. Afterwards he went to Santiago de Compostela and offered a bracelet of his lady's as thanks. Presumably his tactic worked and he escaped his prison of love. When I had finished my drinks, I paid my bill, hoisted my pack onto my back and left. I walked down the main street of what seemed a very clean and well-organized village until I came to the Refugio. As soon as I entered I realized that this was a very special place. I felt comfortable immediately, and the host had a large warm smile to welcome pilgrims. I looked around the courtyard a bit, noticing the showers and multiple sleeping quarters at the rear. The Refugio was spotlessly clean and decorated with plants everywhere.

Courtyard of the refugio at Hopital de Orbigo.

Since it was the middle of the day, I really didn't want to stop here so I asked the proprietor if I could just have lunch and rest for awhile before continuing. He agreed, and proceeded to show me the sleeping quarters. There was a male and female bedroom separated by a walkway with tents set up in the yard at the far end. This is the only time I encountered separate quarters for men and women. Curiously, in the walkway several wild birds had taken to hanging out. They would fly in boldly and sit on the clotheslines that were strung up and sing happily. They seemed to have no fear of pilgrims and to enjoy their role as entertainers. I sat at a table in the courtyard and ate my lunch of fruit, bread and cheese, and then rested for about an hour on one of the bunks in the sleeping quarters. Before leaving I stopped in the office to thank the host and get my passport stamped. There I encountered Alexandro the biologist and his friend who were just checking in.

Towards Astorga.

We greeted each other and spoke for awhile before I put on my pack and started off. At the end of the long straight cobbled street I stopped and turned to look back for a moment and caught a glimpse of Win, the woman I had walked with the day before to Villar de Mazarife, just going into the Refugio. Small world this, el Camino de Santiago. I arrived in Astorga at about 7:30 that evening after a hellish walk mostly on highways. I must have taken a wrong turn somewhere since my guidebook describes a much more interesting walk through fields and forests. In any case, after climbing a steep stair I reached the top of the hill on which Astorga is situated, and checked into the very crowded Refugio. After selecting the only available bunk in a large room crowded with double decker bunks, I went out to look around and get the feel of the city. Astorga was brimming with life. Residents and tourists were walking the streets and enjoying the bars. There is a beautiful promenade park just behind the Refugio that is essentially built on top of the city walls. From there you can look out and see far into the distance toward

Promenade park.

Rabinal del Camino and the highest point of the Camino on Monte Irago where the iron cross, Cruz de Ferro, is situated. Astorga is at 873 meters elevation and within a day and a half walk I would be at the cross, which is at 1,515 meters and 33 km away. Admittedly, I was a bit apprehensive about the steep upward climb and decided at about this point, as I looked out at the mountains I had to cross, to stay an extra night in Astorga and rest up a bit. After Cruz de Ferro the road drops even more steeply than it rose: down to 486 meters at Cacabelos 35 km further on, only to rise steeply again to 1,300 meters at O Cebreiro 35 km later. Definitely cause for some additional rest I reasoned. After a difficult night at the crowded Refugio I was having café solo at the Gaudi Hotel while waiting for a room to be ready. If I hadn't checked with a very ordinary hotel off the plaza a bit earlier, I would feel guiltier about the expense of the room at the Gaudi. The Gaudi was actually less expensive, 5500 pts, and is a very posh well managed place overlooking the plaza and Antonio Gaudi's neo-gothic Bishop's Palace directly across from it, and the Cathedral just to the left. It seemed like the Ritz of Astorga and I really enjoyed the idea of first class service after roughing it on the road. I had to wait for a room because I insisted on one that was at the front of the building overlooking the plaza, the Bishop's Palace and the Cathedral. I thought that if I was going to go in style I should go all the way and get the room with the view I wanted. When the room was ready settled in, took a shower and shaved, and called the concierge to have a few of my clothes cleaned stressing that it must be done very quickly in order for me to leave the following morning. I was also determined to mail the additional weight

I was carrying on to Santiago since the highest points of the Camino were coming up. After carefully sorting out and separating the items I needed from those I would send ahead, I went down to the front desk and asked for an empty box, string and wrapping paper. Of the three items I was able to get only the box, but it was a start, so I packed the box and would wait until tomorrow when the post-office opens to conjure up some wrapping paper

View of the Bishop's Palace from my hotel window.

and string in order to mail the package. Later as I sit in the park with the view of tomorrow's walk I pray that my leg holds up. I must learn to open my heart and just BE, and decide to visit the small church next to the cathedral before dinner. In the church of Santa Maria there is a service taking place which I experienced from the rear of the church along with a magnificent Christ in one of the side alters. As I leave the church I encountered a Frenchman using a copper dosing wand as he searched for energy fields around the exterior of the church. Very strange and he was the object of much curiosity from the people on the street. I walked a few meters into the plaza and stopped into a shop selling pastries, the mantecadas (butter buns) for which Astorga is famous, and asked for a piece of wrapping paper and some string which the clerk very graciously gave me. I was psyched! Finally, I had all the necessary elements to mail this package of heavy items I didn't need, but the final test would be in the post office tomorrow.

Christ figure in the Diocesan Museum.

There is a wonderful Diocesan Museum containing paintings and sculpture located on the left side of the cathedral and since I still had time before any restaurants were open, I decided to visit it. As it turns out it was well worth the price of admission and I spent about an hour soaking in the magnificent works. As I left, I ran into a young woman who had the keys to the museum, and I asked her she would allow me to photograph them since I am always interested in tools of any sort. She enthusiastically agreed and as

Keys to the Diocesan Museum.

I set about making a few photographs, an older man who apparently had something to do with the museum objected strenuously. I suppose he was worried that I intended to make a counterfeit set of keys and rob the place. In the end, the young woman basically told him to shut up and stop obstructing what was obviously a fine art mission in itself. Luckily for me, she was a far better judge of character than her associate—so much for the wisdom of age. Having breakfast at the hotel at 8:00. Like everything else about the Goudi Hotel the restaurant is beautifully put together with an air of substance. After eating, I made my way over to the post office and after much going back and forth with the clerk; he finally communicated which forms needed to be filled out and what the address should be for general delivery in Santiago. I paid the postage and was free of 3.74 kilos, almost 8 pounds, and felt very grateful for it. That much weight will have a significant impact on the feel of my pack, which at this point is about half the weight it was on the day I started. After visiting Banco de Castilla and getting ripped off in the amount of 1000 pts for a commission to exchange my American Express Travelers checks (this despite a prominent sign claiming no commission), I headed over to the cathedral for one last visit. While in the cathedral I remembered the unique scent when the priests walked by me the day before. Quite rare really, and at the time I thought that it was the smell of divinity since it seemed to be coming from the priests and I had never experienced anything like it before. I liked Astorga but I had to continue. I had shed a considerable amount of weight both physically and spiritually having realized how much fear had permeated my life, and was glad to be on the road again.

A corner of the Astorga Cathedral.

July 13–14

Astorga–Rabanal del Camino

Cobbled streets of Castrillo de los Polvazares.

It felt good to be walking again after an extra day's rest in Astorga. I was refreshed both physically and spiritually. In El Ganso I stopped at a bar and had an ice cream and café solo. It was hot, as usual, and I appreciated the cool dark interior of the bar. Just as I was leaving, a group of boisterous pilgrims entered, several couples traveling together. They were very well dressed, I thought, for a pilgrimage, and unusually loud and gregarious. I walked a few meters further and encountered the ruins of a grass roofed huts for which this area is well known according to my guidebook. A bit further I encountered a very amusing Cowboy Bar with its painted exterior and rustic interior. What it had to do with Cowboys escaped me but I stopped for a glass of wine anyway.

Cowboy Bar.

At 5:00 I reached Rabanal del Camino. The Refugio here is operated by an American, Nancy, and her Spanish husband José and is absolutely superb. It is known as the Refugio Gaucelmo, and is actually the old parish house, which has been reconstructed. Situated on a gentle hillside in the center of village, it is ancient yet contemporary in its renovation. Nancy is an anthropologist who is working on her doctoral thesis with el Camino as her subject. We had an interesting conversation and her response to the idea that pilgrims were "less than a full shilling" was that rather than being deficient in some way, they were in transition. Nancy told me that she had taken color photographs for the illustrations in her book and that the publisher really wanted black and white photographs. Due to seriously uninformed technical advice, in my opinion, Nancy actually made the pilgrimage a second time just to reshoot the photographs in black and white. Certainly the color photographs could have been transformed into black and white, especially in this age of the use of digital technology in pre-press systems.

Refugio Gaucelmo.

After checking out the sleeping quarters, which were quite filled to the brim with pilgrims, I wandered down a path and investigated a large utility building, which had two large rooms, one with an actual bed. Of course, being the claustrophobic that I am, I immediately approached my hosts and suggested that I relocate to the shed and free up a bunk in the main house. They agreed to this, and after I set up my sleeping bag on the bed, a couple of cyclists rolled in and took up residence in the other room. I was really quite delighted with my private room, and after washing my socks and shirt, headed up to the restaurant to check it out. Rabanal del Camino was a very busy place, in fact, the village itself was jam packed with pilgrims. I walked down a hill to the lower plaza where there was another bar and hostel, both of which were brimming with pilgrims.

The shed at Refugio Gaucelmo.

At dinner time when I entered the restaurant there wasn't a seat to be had and after a bit I decided to walk up to the top of a hill overlooking the village and watch the sunset. This was a magical experience. The sun set in a glory of color and the field I watched from was unique with clumps of bushes and footpaths. I thought of the distance I had come and the apprehension I felt about tomorrow's walk to the highest point on el Camino marked by the Iron Cross. When I returned to the restaurant it was still overcrowded, and after talking for awhile with Pauline, a French woman, I went back to the Refugio for a dinner of sardines, yogurt, and cheese. I slept well in the shed and at 6:30 A.M. was up having coffee and rolls provided by my hosts. At 7:00

everyone was fussing around preparing to leave, myself included. After saying goodbye to Nancy and José the mountain lay in front of me.

July 15
Rabanal del Camino–Moninaseca

Foncebadon.

The morning was bright and clear as I set off on my uphill trek. After a short bit on a dirt path, el Camino continued on the paved road, winding upward. For awhile I could see the other pilgrims who had left Rabanal at the same time I did up ahead on the road. Eventually I was on my own walking upward on what seemed a freshly paved asphalt two-lane road. I felt better as I walked since it seemed the steepness of the road would not be terribly demanding physically, which turned out to be the case. After about 5 km I reached the ancient ruins of the village of Foncebadón, which I had been looking forward to for quite some time since I had read about it in various pilgrim accounts. I guess I over romanticized it in my imagination because when I walked through the village with its fallen down buildings with thatched roofs, it didn't seem all that magical. As with everything, another day, another year, and my response might have been different. Foncebadón is just off the paved road and its main (and only) street runs parallel for a few hundred meters. According to my guidebook, it was an important stop on the way and appears in records as early as the 10th century. "The hermit Gaucelmo (who died in about 1123) built a hospital and hostelry here for pilgrims crossing the punishing Foncebadón pass."

Prayers and mementoes at the base of Cruz de Ferro.

I took some photographs and was surprised to see that at least one building at the top of the street was inhabited. Why not, I thought, but it must be very lonely. Cruz de Ferro is an iron cross on top of a long wooden pole on top of a large pile of stones. At an elevation of 4512 feet above sea level, it is the highest point on El Camino. As I understand it, tradition holds that pilgrims who add a stone to the pile will have their sins forgiven and join a ritual that predates the Romans. I not only placed a stone for myself, but also for every member of my family. I rested, took a few photographs, and also took a snapshot of a Scandinavian family for them using their camera. While I was very pleased to have reached the summit, it really didn't seem like a momentous event. Perhaps my senses have been dulled by the fatigue and monotony of walking almost every day for the last 25 days. Still, there was no doubt that I had reached a milestone and I was happy to acknowledge that before moving on. I continued on the paved road for a bit and came to a makeshift Refugio of sorts flying a flag with the red cross that I associate with the Knights Templar. As I approached, the host rang a large bell that was hung outside to announce to the spirits that yet another pilgrim (or fool) has managed to climb to this remote spot at the top of a mountain. I entered the encampment, which seemed to be a combination of ancient stone buildings and temporary summer camp, and exchanged greetings with the man in charge. Since I don't speak Spanish we really had little to offer each other but I sat for awhile on one of the benches and rested as I took in what seemed like an eccentric yet welcoming Refugio. I had the feeling that here was a fanatically dedicated proponent of the way of Santiago.

Summit refugio.

If there is a secret cult of the Knights Templar, this man is certainly a chief officer and probably has a radio hidden out back that he uses to communicate with Louis back in Aroyo de San Bol outside of Burgos. There was no evidence of any other pilgrims and my host buried his head in some work at a bench.

While the Cruz de Ferro offered no particular thrill for me, walking along the summit of this pass did. Here, in the rarefied atmosphere of the highest point of an ancient tradition, the mountains themselves came alive and spoke to me. I felt embraced by their presence, as powerful and mysterious as any experience of nature I have ever felt. Now the road began to descend steeply and walking on the paved asphalt that I have been on since leaving

Rabanal became a chore.

As I learned on the second day of my pilgrimage as I descended to Roncesvalles—going down is more painful than going up. A whole new set of little used muscles come into play and they complain bitterly about being

Magical mountains.

pressed into service. After several kilometers el Camino veers off the paved road onto a footpath, which is very challenging. It is a narrow path with loose stones and broken shale ledge that can be very slippery and difficult to negotiate. The fact that I have already come about 13 km since this morning adds considerably to the difficulty I'm sure. About three kilometers before reaching El Acebo the signs started. They were hand painted and attached to a stick hammered into the ground next to the footpath. Every twenty meters or so I came upon a new sign urgently advertising the best bar in Acebo. I must admit that I was a little put off by the blatant advertising, which I had not previously encountered on my pilgrimage. The bar being touted was José's, and being jaded as I am by overexposure to advertising, I was deeply suspicious of the quality of José's bar simply by the presence of the aggressive signage.

Looking back at the loose shale.

I thought no more about it and entered the village and strolled down the main street. About halfway down the street I was accosted by two men who were overly friendly and suggested I stop for refreshments at the bar that was right there. I could hear the music from a radio playing and see the patrons inside the doorway. Quite tired after the arduous descent, I entered the bar and ordered a beer. As I sat I realized there was something a little off about

Looking toward El Acebo.

the place that I instantly disliked. It was owned and operated by a father and his two sons who quarreled constantly as the father lorded over them. I'm not sure if it was the bickering or some other aspect of the bar that made me uncomfortable, but even though was hungry I drank my beer and left immediately. As I went outside the father was working the street, cajoling new arrivals to village to enter his bar. Down at the end of the street was a mural with another advertisement for José's bar and I made the left turn up to a small plaza where the bar was located. As soon as I entered José's I knew I was in the right place. Don José himself was open, warm, and friendly. He understood enough English to get by and we hit it off immediately. It was clear that he loved his bar, serving people and making them happy. Open on a small table in front of the bar was an album filled with postcards and letters from Spain and elsewhere from patrons he had served well. Here is a case where my suspicions about the aggressive advertising were ill founded. I could see why Don José felt the need to advertise since the Brothers Grim up the road did their best to prevent anyone from passing without entering their bar. Also Don José's bar was the second one you come to and it was a few steps off the Camino putting him at a clear disadvantage. I had a brandy outside until the rain came too heavy and I moved inside to a table in the back since there were customers at the two tables in the front room.

Mobile market.

Before going inside, I enjoyed seeing the mobile market pull into the plaza and do business with the women of the village. These trucks service the villages that are too small to have their own market and I had seen variants of this small truck in several villages along the way. Once inside, I ordered the day's special of lentil soup, chicken, fries, and salad with rice pudding for desert. I had several cafés as well and the bill was 750 Pts. The food was delicious and more importantly, I felt relaxed and ready to continue to Molinaseca another 8.5 km. I resolved to send José a postcard from Santiago when I reach it.

Switchback road before Molinaseca.

It continued to rain intermittently as I walked out of El Acebo past the memorial to the pilgrim killed while cycling. Although my guidebook mentions a forge at Compludo it is a 5 km detour which I had no inclination of making. I walked mostly on the road to Molinaseca through beautiful mountains and gorges. The actual marked Camino takes a footpath running parallel to the road, but my feet and legs were so tired from the descent from Monte Irago, that I thought it might be easier though longer due to the switchbacks. The flies were beginning to become a serious bother until I noticed that it was the sweat on my hatband that was attracting them. This meant the end of a comfortable hat that had served me well up to this point. As I entered Molinaseca at 5:30 it began to rain heavily and put my pack down in the covered courtyard of the Capilla de la Virgen and went in and watched a service in progress. This is a fine little chapel and the service gave me a chance to rest for a few moments before crossing the picturesque bridge into Molinaseca proper and checking into the Refugio From Hell at the far end of village. That was my name for this, the most poorly operated Refugio I would encounter. The facility itself is actually quite reasonable and large. There is a large room as you enter the front doors that leads to the shower, toilet facilities, and stairs to the second floor where the bunks are located. On the front and sides of the building there are covered porches. On the day I arrived one side porch was entirely occupied by tents, one tent immediately next to the other. The big problem for an otherwise reasonable system was overcrowding. There were simply too many pilgrims vying for space in an overcrowded facility. I waited my turn to register with the man in charge and after one or two pilgrims ahead of me were checked in and stamped my turn came. I could see that the host was completely overwhelmed, a fact which he freely admitted. He was entirely alone in managing the Refugio. I commiserated with him a bit both out of genuine compassion and also to learn more of the depth of the crisis he was attempting to manage. He assigned me to a spot in one of the tents on the porch and we walked out the front door and around the side so he could show me the exact tent. When we came to the tent he folded over the entry flap and as we both peered in, the stale musty air escaped past us as we gazed upon a tent completely crammed with sleeping bags filled with dozing pilgrims. My heart sank at the prospects of squeezing into this human sardine can, and, incredibly, he started to wake people up and instruct them to move around in order to accommodate my sleeping bag. I told him as firmly as I could to give it up, since I had no intention of squeezing into the tent and I asked about an increasingly attractive spot on the floor between the coat rack and a first aid cabinet. At first he adamantly refused on the basis of access to the cabinet, but eventually gave in after coming to his senses and recognizing the insanity of the situation. By now new pilgrims were being turned back to village to find shelter elsewhere. After staking out my claim to the floor, I checked out the showers and toilets that were filthy with soaked floors. Then I went outside to the porch where there were benches and tables and just sat for awhile watching my overworked host operated a kiosk with beverages and t-shirts. After a short while I decided to do a little sightseeing and walked back to village. I admired the mansions with their coats of arms on the front and the lovely little bridge over the river Meruelo. I was also investigating possible places to eat but didn't see any that suited me. Either they were too formal or just a bar with tapas. I chose the latter, and had a glass of wine and a few assorted tapas in an otherwise deserted bar with a blaring television and bright fluorescent lights. Certainly a big step down from the cordial lunch at Don José's bar in El Acebo but it would have to do. The rain had calmed down and after returning to the Refugio, I watched the lightning over the mountains to the east. The huge pilgrim population of the Refugio had not calmed down, and groups of young people sat around in groups on the front steps long after 11:00 preventing any sleep. They seemed to delight in the locals who stopped by on motorcycles and zoomed off back to village. Eventually, well after midnight, they decided to pack it in and things quieted down. Then at about 2:00 in the morning the overhead lights went on inexplicably. I got up and tried every switch in the building but could not find the one to turn off the lights. I would be leaving here at first light.

July 16

Molinaseca–Cacabelos

Castle of the Knights Templar.

I am up at first light, though I don't think I actually slept in the full sense of the word. I had gotten my gear together last night so I could make a clean and fast break this morning. It feels good to sneak out of the building, stepping over bodies, and trying to be careful not to slam the door. Freedom again at last as I set a quick pace up the street towards Ponferrada and the legendary castle of the nights templar 7 km ahead. At about 7:30 I was standing in front of the castle, which is very impressive and must certainly be the model for Disneyland. Two imposing turrets with high walls all around guard the front door. I spent a couple of hours photographing the structure and was very disappointed in not being able to enter. I had read of three recent accounts by pilgrims who describe buying tickets and exploring the interior of the castle. I asked the woman at the information center when the castle was closed to visitors and she told me that it had never been open. Naturally there was no point in arguing with her, and I was tired after little or no sleep the night before, so I went off in search of breakfast.

View of the castle foundation.

As I sat and drank my café con lèche, I thought about the Templars and the immense power they wielded. This castle was built in the early 11th century and stands as an imposing monument to their wealth and power. The Templars played an important role in the Crusades and afterwards maintained the security and safety of pilgrims in this remote part of the country. By the beginning of the 14th century they were so powerful that it became difficult for kings and popes alike to discipline them. Accordingly, in 1307, trumped up charges were brought against them by King Philip IV of France, their leaders systematically tortured and killed, and by 1312 the Order of the Knights Templar was eradicated. A sad and ignominious ending to a once proud and honorable organization.

Cobblestones, Ponferrada.

I found a supermarket and bought some supplies; my usual hard cheese, bread, a little sausage, and a couple of bottles of water. On my way out of village, I bought three rolls of Fuji 400 film and a package of the amazing second skin bandages that the Norwegians introduced me to for the still painful wounds on my Achilles heels. The way out of Ponferrada was down a road leading to a bridge over the River Sil and then steeply up through a neighborhood of apartment buildings. This was a somewhat rough and dirty section that leads to a far more affluent neighborhood at the top of the hill overlooking the city. Here, I walked through clean, safe streets with attractive houses and well cared for lawns. At this point my right shin tendons were very painful as I walked and I was very concerned about my ability to walk with the pain. Just at the outskirts of village before passing through an underpass I stopped and sat on the wall of a garden to dress my wounds. I took off my right boot and carefully massaged my shin before wrapping it in a bandage. As I sat a French couple came by and asked how I was doing. Being the stoic, I of course told them everything was fine instead of asking them to call for an ambulance. Shortly afterwards, two Frenchmen came by and one asked me,

"How was your sleep?"

"My sleep?" I repeated, having no idea what he was talking about.

"Your walking."

"Not good," I told him.

"How's yours?"

"Horrible!" he said patting his leg as they walked on.

Ponferrada.

The treatment and short rest seemed to help a bit, but the pain was still intense as I walked, so I proceeded slowly and with great deliberation. After a few paces down a paved street, a man on a bicycle stopped me and sent me back to a turnoff I had missed. I really felt as though Santiago himself had intervened on my behalf since I was in no condition to be putting on kilometers in error only to retrace my steps.

Presently I entered a small village, just an intersection really, with a few stores, a bar, and a public phone. The sky was beginning to look very dark and ominous so I decided to pause for a short while and phone my wife Cameron back home north of Boston. We spoke for awhile, and I am always glad to hear her voice. I forget, struggling as I am with my own challenges, how difficult it is for her, having been left alone for an extended period.

A local man comes by and I ask him if he thinks it will rain. He responds: "Possibly no rain," and crosses the street and enters the bar. The sky is getting darker by the second and the lights come on in the bar. It is 2:35 and I head for the bar rather than the expanse of open plain that I can see ahead. The bar is a large long room on the corner of the building. Booths line one side with plate-glass windows and the counter runs the full length of the room opposite the windows. A group of men congregate at the end of the bar toward the front and I take a booth at the rear. After unloading my pack I approach the bar and order a café solo and brandy to ease the pain, and take it back to my table by the window. Then the sky opens up and heavy drenching rain falls in sheets, immediately flooding the streets. I glance over to the "possibly no rain" guy who has apparently forgotten his prediction since he takes no notice. Although this is the heaviest rain I've seen so far, accompanied by steady thunder and lightening, it lightens up after a few minutes and finally stops. I pay my bill, gather my gear, and head out. Every step is painful so I walk slowly for a few kilometers and stop to sit on a bench outside of a house in one of Spain's little ghost villages as I've come to think of them. They apparently were populated until quite recently. The houses show evidence of people having lived in them and the plants are healthy but there is no one around. It is very eerie, as though the entire population of the village were sucked up by an alien spacecraft and abducted. What is more probable is that they are avoiding me like the plague since I am the alien. Then Santiago himself seems to take pity on me in the form of two pilgrims who come toward me. They are wearing shorts and I notice that one has a bandage on his right shin. When they reach me they stop and we chat for a bit since they speak English. I ask the man with the bandage about his injury, and he tells me it is a tendon problem exactly like mine, which he incurred in León, exactly like me. Very weird. He proceeds to tell me that they are from Belgium and that he is a doctor. Then, he gives me very specific instructions about how to apply a bandage that will work, pointing out his own bandage. This information was revolutionary! Really. The doctor in León had no clue about the bandaging technology that was being revealed to me, nor did the pilgrim I spoke to in Burgos who was aborting his pilgrimage due to tendon injury. I was practically dumbstruck in my gratitude. The key to the effectiveness of the Belgian doctor's bandage lie in not simply wrapping the shin with an elastic as is typically done, but rather, three pieces of bandage scientifically applied. First off, you must use a non-stretch adhesive bandage several inches wide, the type that is typically used to hold a bandage on. The first piece is placed on the front of the shin from knee to ankle. Just a straight piece running up and down with no wrapping around. Then, a second piece is wrapped tightly around the ankle, overlapping the first piece of bandage. Finally, the third piece is wrapped tightly around the shin just below the knee. When applied correctly, the unbearable pain you experienced vanishes. Somehow, this particular wrapping procedure holds the tendons and muscles in place and you are almost as good as new. The bandages must be very tight—as tight as possible without cutting off circulation. It was 4:00 and the doctor's friend was getting anxious and wanted to continue. We all shook hands and after I thanked him earnestly, the continued on to Villafranca. The doctor had very caring eyes, a sign to me that he was obviously in the right profession.

After a boring walk on a paved road, I arrived in Cacabelos at 6:30 P.M. I had gotten out of phase with the daily walks in my guidebook, which neatly maps the route in walk able segments of 20 to 35 km with stops in villages and cities with Refugios for pilgrims. This was not a problem today but would soon become one. I had a beer in a central bar and asked about the Refugio, which was over the river at the far end of village and out in the fringe area. This sounded too much like the Refugio I stayed in last night in Molinaseca so when I saw an advertisement for Hostel de Santa María, I went for it. The word hostel used to describe it was somewhat misleading, since it turned out to be a splendid recently renovated hotel. The room was new and clean and cost 3500 Pts., relatively expensive, but I really needed a decent night's rest and felt no guilt at all about passing over the Refugio. After taking care of my laundry and relaxing I went to dinner at a fine restaurant, the Meson, a few doors up the street. I ordered roast pork, fish soup, and rice pudding and thoroughly enjoyed it. Back at the hostel, I redressed my sore tendon with the bandages I bought yesterday. The bandage cost a fortune, 1400 Pts.., since in Spain, any medical supplies must be purchased at an actual pharmacy or apothecary where prices are high since there is no other option. I was really shocked by the price, since it was easily twice what I would expect to pay back home, even after taking into consideration the currency conversion. In America, for example, you can buy bandages in a variety of places ranging from the pharmacy to K-Mart

View from my room at Hostel Santa María in Cacabelos.

to a food supermarket, and the prices are low and competitive. As I settled in for the night it was becoming clear that something had gone awry in the gastronomic department. I wasn't feeling well and apparently something I ate or drank did not agree with me, and the condition was exacerbated by the smell of fresh paint wafting up from the recently renovated lobby of the hostel. Still, tomorrow would be a new day, and, I hoped, one where I would throw off the queasiness I felt as I went to sleep.

July 17
Cacabelos–Ambascasas

Puerta del Perdon, west portal.

The morning is bright and clear as I cross the River Cúa on my way out of Cacabelos. I stop on the far side at a bar for café con lèche (grande) before continuing up the road and at 1:30 in the afternoon I arrive in Villafranca del Bierzo. My stomach is still very delicate, and, in fact, worse than when I started. The first stop I make just before entering the village is at the Church of Santiago with its elegantly carved north portal, the Puerta del Perdón. The Spanish Pope, Calixto III (1455-1458) must have had me in mind when he granted a concession to pilgrims to stop here if they were unable to continue and receive all the privileges of a pilgrim who makes it to Santiago de Compostela. I took a few photographs of the little church and some details of the Portal itself, which is very worn, and weather beaten. After sitting in the church for a few moments to collect my thoughts, I proceeded down the hill and into the village itself. Villafranca is a picturesque little village perched in a river valley with steep mountains to the west directly in my path. I must say that here I had serious doubts about my ability to continue. I felt sick and the road ahead seemed particularly challenging. At one point as I crossed the main street, the Norwegian pilgrim sprang out of his seat at a café and came over to greet me. We spoke for a moment and it was good to see a familiar face as I girded myself for the trek ahead. Finally, feeling slightly dazed and ill, but having no intention of spending the night in Villafranca, I bolstered all my courage and started out.

My guidebook tells me I have two choices:
1. Take the road along the busy paved highway, which is unpleasant and very dangerous due to the traffic but is the authentic route of el Camino.
2. Follow the new route up the Cerro del Real, which is more demanding, but goes through unspoiled countryside.

Having no idea what possessed me, I took the right fork and started up the unbelievably steep path to the top of the mountain. Part of my decision, I'm sure, was my dislike of smelling diesel exhaust from the trucks, which, in my condition, would surely sicken me more. Before making this decision I could see that this stretch of road was indeed heavily trafficked. In any case, up I went, feeling a lot like a mountain goat, except that I stopped every few meters to rest. Once at the top, the footpath followed the crest of the ridge through low scrub brush. If I thought that being up here would be less of a assault on my olfactory senses I was wrong. It seems that much of the mountaintop has been burned off for some reason, either by lightening or intentionally, and the odor of burnt brush was everywhere and pungent. As I walked the narrow path I could look to my left and see the road far down in the valley. I could make out pilgrims walking along in groups by the side of the road and the traffic they were confronting. Up here, I was completely alone. Not another soul in sight since I left Villafranca. I felt like I was walking along in an alternative dimension, disconnected yet part of normal reality since I could see it far in the distance. This feeling was heightened when I walked under the high tension electric lines crossing the path. They hissed and crackled with raw electricity emphasizing the feeling that I was in a place that was distinctly not normal and that I probably shouldn't be here. I realized that I was running low on water, which is always a problem in the hot sun when working so hard physically so I conserved my water as much as possible but began to feel sicker with every step. This was without question the most difficult part of the entire Camino for me. Not just because I was physically challenged, beyond tired, hurting, and dangerously low on food and water. I had experienced all of that before. But somehow, up here on the desolate ridge, the combination of circumstances conspired to defeat my spirits for the first time. I felt lonely and afraid and could only equate it to the way Christ must have felt in the desert. I had sank to the depths and felt abandoned by all, even God. This was a level of despair I have never felt before. I passed the time by delving deep into rooms in my psyche that I know I have created, and that remain closed, secretive, and are sources of pain and fear. As I walked I remembered what Win had told me about concentrating on her heart and having ecstatic experiences and I concentrated on mine, flooding it with silver light, not for ecstasy, but just to remain afloat. I beseeched everything that I held dear to accompany me and protect me on this internal journey. I called upon all of my guides and shamanic spirits to come along, and as I opened one room after another, I forced myself to openly confront whatever the contents. I encountered much unfinished business that strongly influences my life in one way or another. As I passed through a room, the knights, who are priests, enter and sanctify it with bells, holy water, and incense, acknowledging that what was buried has been brought into the light.

Detail, Puerta del Perdon, north portal.

I opened other doors, and rooms appeared with a spectrum of experiences that I did my best to at least acknowledge. After awhile I had to give up on this inner work since it simply became too draining on top of the physical demands. My pilgrimage is becoming as much an inner journey as an outer one. Ever since my dream about receiving an award but having slept through it, I am constantly asking myself if I am awake, and what exactly does being awake mean anyway? When I descended from the mountain completely out of water and feeling more despairing than ever, the path joined a paved road that I followed for several kilometers. Still feeling quite sick and unsteady in addition to being almost blown over by the large trucks rushing past, I came around a curve and saw a roadhouse, or motel just up ahead. I felt as though I had been saved since I didn't think I could go on much longer. It was dusk, and I had been trudging a difficult path for about 10 hours though covering only about 25 km since Cacabelos. I sat at a table and ordered a beer since I was too sick to even think about eating, and was beginning to think that I might have gotten sun poisoning in addition to everything else. I watched as two older pilgrims entered and appeared to be just as relieved as I to have come upon this haven for truckers. After a few minutes of resting I approached the bartender and arranged for one of the rooms located through a door in an adjoining part of the building. The room was not much bigger than a closet with a single bed, bureau, and a bathroom. For me, however, it was paradise and after washing my socks and showering I was asleep almost immediately.

July 18
Ambascasas–O Cebreiro

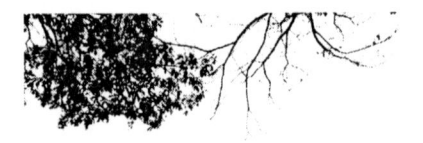

View from the path.

I am having coffee and croissants. Feeling tired and dispirited but must continue even though yesterday's haul broke me. After a short bit on the highway, the trail veered off to a pleasant road through picturesque villages just before it begins to climb steeply toward O Cebreiro at 3879 feet, almost as high as Cruz de Ferro. At the last village before the trail rose steeply, leaving civilization behind, I stopped at a shop selling very expensive fruit and bought an orange. I ate it outside the shop on a wall by the road enjoying the other pilgrims passing by on their way up the trail. After savoring the orange for as long as possible I set out. This part of the journey was really

Looking back.

quite stunning. The trail was beautiful, just a cart track really, bordered with a stone wall on one side over which enchanted vistas came into view. After a couple of hours of climbing I was exhausted and lay down on the top of the stone wall and had a nap for half an hour. After continuing and reaching the higher portion of the trail where it began to level off, I looked back at the magical expanse of villages and mountains that I had just traveled through. The view was spectacular.

Before long I came to the stone marking the entrance to Galicia, a moment I had been anticipating for days since it signified the beginning of the last leg of el Camino. Santiago is located in Galicia, the northwestern-most region of Spain. After trudging along further, I arrived at what I hoped was the village of O Cebreiro. That fact, however, was not immediately clear to me when I came upon a large walled in lawn where young people were setting up tents and I could smell food cooking in a nearby kitchen. Since it looked very much like a Refugio to me, I entered the building and asked. I was told that this was not the Refugio and to continue down the road a few meters. As I left the compound, which turned out to be the back

Galicia marker.

of the Church of Santa María la Real, I was still baffled by the large number of young people setting up tents. As I came to learn later, this was an organized tour group from Britain traveling with two vans that carried their tents and packs from one stop to the next. The center of village was a few steps down the road around a turn, and consisted of just a few buildings really. An ethnography museum is housed in two of the pallozas. These are round buildings with straw roofs that exemplify a prehistoric tradition. Later when I explored the interiors they felt very dark and eerie.

Pallozas.

The center of village has two bars, which are also restaurants. One is in the upper section of the village and the other is in the lower section near the road that passes through. When I finally reached the Refugio it was closed and scheduled to open shortly. It is a modern building on two levels and quite large, designed to accommodate 80 pilgrims. The views from the grounds of the Refugio down into the valley below are breathtaking. Many pilgrims were standing and sitting around passing the time waiting for the Refugio to open. When it finally did, there was an immediate line crushing in upon the overwhelmed host who sat at a desk taking names, stamping passports, and assigning sleeping areas. Before long, 152 pilgrims had signed in. As I waited my turn I had a chance to peek at the guest register and noted that 250 pilgrims had been accommodated the night before. Every available space was taken. People were sleeping in the halls and on the floor in the kitchen in addition to the beds. I was assigned to sleep on the floor in a large room with about 40 people. Now I was seriously regretting having left my

Refugio at O Cebreiro.

sleeping pad behind since a sleeping bag by itself simply isn't enough padding on the hard floor. Still, I was happy to have a spot on the floor especially after hearing the stories of pilgrims who were forced to sleep in one of the pallozas, which had only hay on the ground. Not that that in itself was so bad, but it turned out that the hay was infested with something that made the next few days unpleasant for the unfortunate pilgrims. El Camino was getting more and more crowded with pilgrims with each passing day as I got closer to my destination of Santiago de Compostela. The reason for this was that groups of young people as well as individuals with limited time were beginning their journey a few days walk from Santiago. The effect was the overcrowded Refugios making it more and more difficult to find a bed.

Central Cebreiro.

As I walked down to the bar in the center of village I encountered the Norwegian couple who were always smiling and happy to talk. We chatted for awhile, discussing the difficulties and perils of el Camino. They told me that many people had hired a porter to transport their gear up to O Cebreiro from the base of the ascent. A very enterprising local was doing a brisk business by hauling pilgrims' packs up in his old car for a few Pts., saving them the burden of carrying their packs up the steep track. Later I heard several pilgrims grumbling and carrying on about the porter who turned up very late. I sat in the bar having a beer and relaxing before exploring the ancient church and the curious round buildings. Up at the top of the hill was the church of Santa María la Real that was quite lovely. Inside are kept the Chal

Sunrise.

ice and Paten commemorating the Miracle of Cebreiro, a 14th century legend which tells of a peasant from a neighboring village who braved a terrible snow storm to receive communion at Cebreiro. The officiating monk was secretly very annoyed with the simple peasant for taking the trouble to come through the storm, when suddenly, the sacramental bread and wine turned literally into the flesh and blood of Christ inside the paten and chalice.

When I returned to the Refugio I ran into Roman, a pilgrim whom I had first met in Burgos. He is making the pilgrimage on a bicycle and had already been to Santiago and was returning to his native Switzerland. We sat in the kitchen and he shared the noodles he was preparing with me while he told me his story. He had spent the last two years as a Swiss guard in Rome guarding the Vatican and was about to enter college upon returning to Switzerland. Unfortunately, he was feeling quite ill with some kind of stomach malady and spent much of the time condemning the Benedictine monks at Samos for refusing to put him up and take care of him.

Roman.

Roman was particularly miffed since it is part of the Benedictine code of ethics to provide hospitality. After talking with Roman for awhile, the strain of the day's journey up the mountain was beginning to wear on me and I headed for my small section of floor, spread out my sleeping bag and was asleep in minutes.

When I awoke at sunrise at least two things were new:
1. The valleys below were filled with fog literally illustrating the fact that we were high up in the clouds. Not only was this beautiful in its own way, but it was interesting in that it was such a dramatic trans-

formation of the scene from the night before.

2. I felt like I had been beaten with sticks. Apparently sleeping on a hard floor did not agree with my skeleton and I had bruised my hip, a condition that would prove to be increasingly painful and troublesome over the next few days.

Tired author at sunrise.

July 19
O Cebreiro– Triacastela

I hooked up with Roman for breakfast. He was off to the east on his way home to Switzerland and I was continuing west to my destination of Santiago de Compostela. We went to the lower restaurant and had coffee and rolls and talked for awhile before departing in opposite directions. For a few kilometers the Camino follows the paved road then breaks off to a dirt path and climbs steeply to the top of Alto de San Roque. At the top there is a small restaurant where most pilgrims stopped to rest and refresh themselves after the hard, steep climb.

Looking back down the path.

I rested here and drank an Orangina, grateful for the sturdy staff I had purchased from the gift shop in St. Jean-Pied-de-Port where I started. This walking stick has been invaluable on many occasions, and I say that without exaggeration. There were sections of the Camino that I literally could not have negotiated without this trusted companion. This staff is made of a hard wood that I can't identify, but it is straight and cut from a branch with a knurled joint forming the top where you hold it. It is exactly 4 feet long (121 cm) with a hole near the top where a leather strap runs through it. Down the length of the staff is inscribed "St. Jean-Pied-de-Port" with ornamental flower patterns on either side. It is stained a lovely brown color and tapers slightly towards the tip, which has a substantial metal point attached.

Detail of engraving on staff.

It is just the right thickness and weight, and is, for all practical purposes, indestructible. All in all, it is a perfect walking stick and I was pleasantly surprised to find such a substantial item sold as a tourist's souvenir at a gift shop. While I have occasionally forgotten it here and there along the way, I always noticed its absence and retrieved it before going no more than a few steps. I truly appreciated having it, especially as I sat recovering after the steep climb up a dirt path with loose rocks.

My bruised hip was getting seriously painful as the day's journey progressed. I became oblivious to the historical and architectural aspects of el Camino and had to focus on simply getting from one place to another, wondering if my abused body would hold up. Thankfully, with the exception of a couple of short steep climbs, the walk from O Cebreiro was mostly downhill and very pleasant with beautiful views.

Ancient tree marks the way.

I actually felt joy for a second or two before my head got in the way as usual.

At 2:00 P.M. I arrived in Triacastela 19.5 km from O Cebreiro. As I entered the village, I walked right past the Refugio which had approximately 60 backpacks lined up outside. I didn't even need to consider staying there after my experience on the floor last night. I knew I was heading for a room with a bed. I checked into the first hostel I came to which was down the end of a street to the right of the Camino. The hostel was over a bar, as usual, but since el Camino had suddenly become so crowded with students, I didn't want to take any chances with not finding a place to stay, so I accepted the first room offered. The room was adequate with a shower down the hall, and after washing up, I went out to a small market and bought some cheese, bread, tuna fish, and olives for dinner. The walls of my hostel were paper thin and the bar downstairs became increasingly loud as pilgrims gathered and celebrated.

At 8:30 it is a beautiful night with a full moon rising. Earlier, I was planning to go to a restaurant but decided that I couldn't face it alone, having become suddenly depressed. My heart is still closed off, and the language barrier combined with the people laughing and having fun downstairs in the bar serves to dramatically emphasize that fact. Physical inventory: groin muscles very painful today. Heels are OK now thanks to the second skin bandages. Tendon has been fine since the Belgian doctor's bandaging advice.

I just took off the bandages after my shower after wearing them for three days. Tomorrow I will try to walk without the bandage. Hip and ribs are sore from sleeping on the floor last night. At midnight the bar downstairs is raging. I close my window to keep out the smell from the bar's grille vent, which is just below and attempt to sleep.

July 20
Triacastela– Sarria

At 8:30 A.M. I am eating little commercially prepared wrapped cakes and café solo in the hostel bar. A native with a surprisingly deep voice that sounds like it is coming from a gravel pit is drinking whiskey and coffee. Meanwhile the French couple leaves with a friend they hooked up with and who is wearing a comical beanie cap with an umbrella sticking up from the center to shade him from the sun.

Leaving Triacastela.

El Camino follows the road leaving Triacastela and criss-crosses it, more or less, all the way to Samos. The trail is very pleasant, and as it descends into Samos, there is a marvelous view of the ancient Benedictine monastery, which was originally founded in the 6th century. This is the very same monastery that Roman, the Swiss Guard, was so upset by—having refused

Stone cross at Samos.

him shelter in his time of need. I arrived in time to hear the bell ringing that announced the noon Mass, and outstanding bell ringing it was. The bells rang for what seemed like half an hour with such great intensity and variation; it was like a concert in itself. Before the Mass I visited the very serious gift shop, not large, but well organized with great variety of merchandise. The monk in charge is very impressed with my staff and asks to see it. After I hand it to him he handles it, inspecting it closely. I can see the businessman wheels turning in his head:

"How much did you pay for it?" he asks.

"60 francs," I tell him.

"But what is the exchange rate?"

"I'm sorry, but I have no idea."

He turns it over a few more times admiring the engraving where it says, St. Jean Pied-de-Port, and hands it back to me approvingly. I left the gift

Monastery at Samos. Note the scallop iron work fence.

shop and hurried up to the church to attend the Mass, which was about to begin. The church interior is impressive with the organ bellowing loudly and shaking the building. Officiating are nine priests dressed in green and white robes with the priest in the center wearing a red sash. They stand behind a long table. The event is as impressive as any well practiced theater complete with alchemic hand movements. At times the center priest holds up both hands as in the experience of an epiphany, while the four priests on each side hold sometimes one, and sometimes both their hands out as in a blessing. Throughout the ceremony a life-size statue of Fruela I stands with raised

Disney at Samos.

sword ready to take your head, while Alfonso II stands on a decapitated head opposite. This was a very moving experience and a welcome rest from the endless walking. After the Mass, the same monk I spoke with earlier about my staff tells me to hurry down for a tour of the cloisters. I rush downstairs just as the tour is starting eager to join when another monk stops me and tells me I need to buy a ticket. At this extension of their marketing prowess, I leave and head up to the village stopping in a bar for a beer before continuing on to Saria, 12 km further. As I reflect on the experience, it occurs to me that Samos is very much like a Disney movie set carefully orchestrated by the Benedictines. It was probably the unnatural cleanliness of the village, almost sterile, coupled with what seemed like an out of place German inn standing next to the monastery that gave me that impression. Outside of town, I am halfway up a dirt track after (gratefully) turning off the paved

Stairs entering Sarria.

road, when a local resident on the road below begins yelling to me that I am going the wrong way. I am really rather dubious, but what do I know? Here's a man who looked to be at least 100 years old and had probably lived here all his life insisting that I am going the wrong way. Reluctantly, I turn around and retrace my steps to the road below where I turned off. I carefully check the sign that clearly indicates that I had taken the correct road. Nevertheless, I defer to the wisdom of the ancient resident and proceed along the literally stinking road. As in many instances along the way, el Camino follows a very similar route to the paved road, and sometimes is a dirt track adjacent to it, and other times joins the road. With this knowledge I proceeded, confident that either way I would reach my destination, Sarria, which I did at 5:30 P.M. After laboring up a long staircase leading to the upper part of village, I found the Refugio without any trouble. It turned out to be full, however, and I was directed further up the Calle Mayor to a hostel half way up the hill. This was a fine place to stay, with the usual bar below and a small market directly across the street. The room I was given was on the second floor overlooking the street with double doors opening to tiny balcony. The host, who was also the bartender, spent at least 15 minutes meticulously explaining how to operate the propane hot water system. He wanted to make very certain that I understood exactly how to turn it off. The room was directly next to the bath with a shower and cost 1000 Pts.—couldn't be more reasonable. After unpacking a few things and a shower, I went across the street to buy food and a bar of soap to wash my clothes. I had to cut a small piece off the bar of soap since it was far too big to carry whole. As I was hanging my socks on the balcony railing to dry, I looked down and there was the Norwegian couple walking down the street. I hailed them and we spoke for a few minutes. They too, were staying in a hostel down the road, and it was great to see them again. It is interesting that for all the times we have met, always at a stopping point, we have never run into each other on the Camino itself, and so have never actually walked together. Still, I feel like we are friends since we have spoken so often and both have children involved with computers. They are always positive and uplifting and I enjoy talking with them. I decided to leave at sunrise so I went down to the bar to pay my bill in advance. There were only a few customers and the bartender was very cordial. After that it was back to my room to read my guide for awhile before sleeping.

Hostel at Sarria.

July 21

Sarria– Ventas de Naron

As planned, the next morning I was on my way at sunrise, heading up to the top of Calle Mayor and past the modern buildings and residential neighborhood. The Way proceeded over a river and across tracks before continuing on through the beautiful Gallician countryside. It felt good to be in Gallicia where my wife and I had visited three years earlier, staying with friends in Santiago de Compostela. It was then that I first learned about the pilgrimage, though it was only a dim recognition at first. It took the intervening years for the idea of actually making the pilgrimage myself to mature into a reality. But because I had been here before it felt like returning home, in addition to Gallicia being the final destination of the pilgrimage.

At about 9:30 A.M. I stopped at a picturesque little inn for coffee and cold toast served by the grumpiest people I had encountered so far. I met with a young couple, guests at the inn, who were just on their way out and we talked for awhile. They were on vacation from professional jobs and were making only part of the pilgrimage like so many who have time constraints. This, incidentally, was the first really bad coffee I had been served in all of Spain. I was shocked, having taken for granted the excellent café solo

Stone inn.

available at any local bar, fresh brewed by the cup. This weak light brown liquid was neither fresh nor brewed by the cup, but created somehow in a pot many hours before. I was very disappointed since I had left Sarria before anything was open and was looking forward to café con lèche. I left the grumpy innkeepers and continued on my way, amazed by the unique antiquity of the stone buildings I past. This was farm country to be sure, and the pungent odor of cow manure permeated the air emphasizing that fact. It was everywhere, not just as I past a barn or farmhouse, but it was so strong and constant that it seemed like the whole area was inside a cow barn. After a few more hours I was actually feeling nauseous from the strong odor. At about 12:30 I stopped at a farm that had transformed one of its buildings into a restaurant and tried again for a decent café con lèche, and to my amazement, was served the same pathetic excuse for coffee I had at the inn. I gave up on the idea of having decent coffee that morning, not that I had any choice. This part of el Camino often consists of a cart track bordered by stone walls on both sides and it was along one of these tracks that I first encountered

Pleasant path in Galicia.

equestrian pilgrims. It was quite a surprise really, and exciting. From out of nowhere a group of riders appeared led by a man with a leather vest who was leading another horse. The group moved fast and before I knew it I was pinned against the stone wall worried that I might be trampled. They passed me, horses slipping and sliding on the track with deep ruts cut by carts, and loose rocks, but moving steadily at a brisk walk and were out of sight as quickly as they appeared. There were about ten riders of various ages, from teenagers to middle aged adults. We exchanged brief greetings as they passed, and they seemed seriously intent upon the business at hand. On that particular stretch of road, it looked like a chore to stay in the saddle with the horses moving quickly on the precarious track. Later I learned that the group had traveled all the way from the Basque country on horseback. I had also noticed that many of the larger Refugios had stables, but this was

Slate, a regional specialty.

the first time I actually saw the horses. I decided that I was much happier moving at a snails pace on foot than bouncing around on the back of a horse. Eventually I came to Portomarín and the great modern bridge leading to the new city. The old Portomarín was submerged when the river Miño was transformed into a reservoir in 1956, and only the highest parts of the ancient architecture protrude from the water's surface. After crossing the bridge, I encountered a pilgrim who informed me that the Refugio was full, as was the hostel. Not exactly great news since I had already walked more than 20 km, but I didn't like the look of the new city perched high on a hill overlooking the river anyway, and was not really too disappointed about having to continue. A few steps from the bridge I stopped at a gasoline station for a short rest and refreshment. Here I bought a can of Coke from a woman who was dressed for a photographic fashion shoot with fastidiously applied makeup to match her outfit. I asked her for water to fill my bottle and was refused. I was shocked, and I must admit, had very un-pilgrim like feelings for her. She dismissed me telling me that she didn't have any water but that there was a public fountain a few kilometers up the road. Then she returned to her impeccably manicured little house right next door to the gas station. No water was actually quite a serious matter since when I walk carrying a pack I need constant water to keep from becoming dehydrated and I was just about out of the precious liquid. But having little choice, I continued. At this point el Camino crosses the river Torres via a footbridge and proceeds around the side of Monte San Antonio. However, after carefully studying my map, I decided to skip the scenic route and proceed directly along the road I was on towards Ventas de Naron, another 13 km further. I made this decision in the interest of preserving my remaining strength since

I reasoned that the road, though boring, would be the shortest and least arduous route. Off I went, trudging along the road towards Ventas de Naron—uphill every step of the way. About halfway there, I reached a rest area with a fountain that ran with terrible tasting undrinkable water. At this point I met Juan from Madrid and we walked together from there to Ventas de Naron.

Ancient farm track and rockpile.

A few steps past the fountain we came to a business or government installation of some sort, all fenced in and very secure. Happily, there was a soft drink machine with cold drinks accessible so we stopped and rested for awhile enjoying our drinks. A kilometer or so further we came to a rather new looking Refugio, which seemed very uninviting for some reason. Here it was, directly on the road, basically in the middle of nowhere—it seemed strange. I went in to use the washroom and fill my water bottle and found a lone pilgrim staying there. He seemed just about as strange as the Refugio itself so Juan and I kept on walking. Actually, the place was so weird that we never even entertained the thought of staying there.

Farm shed.

As I walked the last 10 km I thought of an open heart. One that weighed in lightly with no worries. This gave me some much needed strength to continue. Suddenly I was overcome with the desire to live closer to the land and to have a farm with chickens, horses, and other animals somewhere in Vermont. Obviously, due to sheer exhaustion, I had flipped. I never before had any such longings, but the feeling was real and stemmed, I thought, from having been so close to the earth for longer than I ever have before. I tried to picture myself returning home and explaining our new life to my wife. How we were going to sell everything quit our jobs and move way up north to the country. Then, in my minds eye, I saw the look of fear and pity in her eyes as she tried to remember where the closest mental hospital was. I knew I had to pull myself together, and that in reality I would last only about a week on a farm. At about 9:00 P.M. I arrived at Ventas de Naron, some 37 km (23 miles) from Sarria where I started 14 hours earlier. This was a long day for me and I was exhausted. Finding the Refugio was easy— it is directly on the road

Horrero for drying grain.

entering the village I went in and claimed a bunk. The place was packed with pilgrims. Apparently everyone shared my feelings about the creepy Refugio back at Gonzar. After dropping off my pack, I ventured the few steps into village and sat down at a table at the only restaurant. This was a tiny place with two tables right on the street and run by a very cordial and happy couple. At the other table sat Philip, the Canadian, whom I have been running into on and off since Roncesvalles, another Canadian, and the New Zealander, Nick. My new acquaintance, Juan, turned up and shared my table. I ordered a tortilla and the host told me that she had used up her last eggs but would go to a neighbor and borrow some, which she did. I was very grateful, and after a grand dinner, returned to the Refugio and found my bunk. That night I had a dream that my father came to a class I was teaching. I had the feeling that he was proud and loving—the opposite of how he was when he was alive.

July 22
Ventas de Naron– Melide

San Xulian do Camino.

I awoke early as usual, and when I stood up the pain in my hip was so intense that I almost fell over. I had to hold on to the bunk as I accessed the searing pain paralyzing me. The consequences of sleeping on the hard floor at O Cebreiro were apparently just coming into full flower. I swallowed my last ibuprofen and began walking. It was very painful at first, but after awhile, the ibuprofen kicked in and I could manage more or less normally. At 1:00 I reached Palas de Rei where I immediately bought a package of twelve 400 mg tablets of ibuprofen for 395 Pts. In the U.S. ibuprofen is packaged as 250 mg pills and larger by prescription only. Needless to say, I was delighted to find the somewhat larger dosage readily available. As I sat in a restaurant in the center of village, I had lunch of a tortilla and wine while I contemplated walking the 14 km to Mellide where my guide says the the following about the Refugio:

"Beautifully built, magnificent refuge that offers all the necessary facilities. 130 beds and stables facilities."

Sounded too good to pass up, and after finishing lunch and watching the world go by for a few minutes, I hobbled onward. I must admit that

San Xulian.

despite the pain, I very much enjoyed walking in Gallicia. The track is often perfectly idyllic, a good surface and lined or arched with tall poplar trees or hedges. I was fortunate also, in that it remained relatively sunny in a region renowned for rain and dampness. A few kilometers outside of Palas de Rei

I stopped for a moment to rest and photograph the beautiful little 12th century parish church of San Xulian do Camino. The legend is that Julian, a soldier, accidentally kills his parents and builds a hospital to repent for his sins. After running the hospital with his wife he is visited by an angel who tells him that he has been granted divine pardon. At 6:30 P.M. I reached Mellid feeling tired and with my hip still hurting, but glad to have made it. The main intersection was a busy place with a little park off to the side. I stopped in a bar on the park to rest and celebrate my arrival. It has a single narrow

Detail, San Xulian.

room with the bar on the left as I entered and with disco music blaring from the stereo competing with the T.V. I took a seat where I could look out toward the street and the park beyond and ordered a café solo and a brandy (for medicinal purposes). At that moment the universe came together in one of those rare moments of magic. The cacophony

Entering Melide.

of the stereo, T.V., traffic, and children yelling in the park collided to form a unified and perfectly syncopated drama with every element moving in elegant synchronicity. Chaos was transformed into harmony. After finishing my drinks I broke the spell and proceeded to the main intersection where I asked for and received directions to the Refugio that was at the end of a side street busy with people and shops. This Refugio was, in fact, quite grand. Except for being overrun with pilgrims it seemed everything that was promised by my guide and more. It was new and well designed with a large kitchen and adjacent dining room. It felt large and spacious and after checking in with the young woman registering new arrivals, I was directed upstairs to select a bunk. Upstairs there were several rooms off the foyer, all large and bright. I selected a lower bunk near the showers and proceeded to unpack and settle in. The first order of business, as usual, was to wash my socks, spare shirt, and underwear, and get them on a line drying as soon as possible. After a shower and a short rest I ventured out to take a look at Mellid. This was a bustling little city filled with life and I was impressed with the unself-conscious way it seemed to host the tourists and pilgrims alike. At the end of a street near the center of village where I entered the city, I came to a plaza lined with shops and the parish church. I entered the church and was absolutely astonished by a small alcove on the left of the main aisle elegantly decorated with faux marble columns. I sat for a moment and listened to the service in progress before returning to the plaza where I bought a small hand towel in one of the shops. Delighted with my simple evening excursion, I returned to the Refugio and ran into the Canadians eating their dinner in the dining room where I joined them and opened a can of sardines I bought back in Triacastela. After we cleaned up I went outside just as the sun was dropping below the horizon, and I retired to my bunk to read for a few minutes before dropping off to sleep.

July 23

Melide– Santa Irene

This morning I woke in the worst pain ever. Far worse than the previous morning, which I didn't think was possible, but here I was literally unable to stand. This was truly amazing. Here I was after 36 days of walking almost every day, and suffering more than ever. After taking two ibuprofen tablets on an empty stomach, I rolled up my sleeping bag and got my pack together holding on to the bunk and whatever else was handy. Gradually, moving very slowly and using my staff more as a crutch than a walking stick, I made my way downstairs and started off towards the main plaza. I limped and hobbled to the nearest open bar that also happened to be the bus station. At this point I thought that I had little choice but to see a doctor or go to a hospital. This was bad and I was very worried. As I sat in the bar having a café con lèche (grande) and a croissant, I thought of how horrible it would be to have come this far and not make it to my destination. I was getting very depressed about it and the thought of taking a bus the final 50 kilometers was even more depressing though definitely an option since I was sitting in a bus station. In my present condition, however, walking was not an option. As the T.V. pumped out American MTV, which was actually quite comforting, I ordered a second café con lèche and sat wondering what to do next. Then, suddenly the drug kicked in and the pain was gone! I was amazed and grateful for the miracle of drugs, and it really was a miracle. Even though I had been taking ibuprofen for days and had a good idea of its capabilities, I never expected this level of instant cure. Pain gone, I asked the bartender to fill my water bottle, which he kindly did, and off I went.

Stately eucalyptus trees line the path.

By now it was 9:30 and I was walking slowly and cautiously with only a slight limp. The track is very friendly for the most part, passing through eucalyptus woods and over streams. At 11:00 I stopped in a tiny hamlet and had a café solo at the bar. I walked out of the bar and was a few steps down the road I had been traveling when a woman carrying a shovel over her shoulder stopped me and asked if I was going on el Camino. I said yes, I was, and she pointed me back in the opposite direction to a left turn just at the other side of the bar. I thanked her profusely, since she had saved me considerable time and effort. This was one of many instances where a kindly native has taken the trouble to straighten out this bumbling pilgrim and I was very grateful. Within a few steps I came upon a fountain with water rapidly

Stream crossing.

flowing from a pipe. As I approached it a rooster crowed and I heard the water splashing into the basin of the fountain. Time stopped. Where was the water that flowed from the fountain? Where was the sound of the rooster? I was transfixed in an instant of clarity between thoughts. Time is a lie. There is no Now. There is no Then. Only the heart can know. I realized for a fraction of a second that trying to be in the present is as futile and as much a lie as living in the past and future. All these thoughts are products of the mind, which is incapable of understanding. Even Ram Dass' famous admonition to "Be here now," is buying into the lie and is futile. As I write these words today, they serve only as vague and inadequate references to a state of consciousness that I am not now experiencing, and, I presume, may not communicate the revelation that I had to those who read this. Yet, I remember the experience, what it means, and how important it is to me, so it's only fair to report it, no matter how inadequately. At 2:30 I walked into Arzua thinking lunch. As I came to the main part of the business section just before the village center, everyone stopped to look at an amazing spectacle: a troop of pilgrims on horseback with hoofs clattering on the pavement, proudly stepping through village at a rapid gait. People came out of the shops and bars to look, wave, and cheer. It was beautiful. These were the same riders I had encountered two days earlier. They must be stopping for extended rests, probably for the sake of the horses, since they are holding my snails pace. At the main intersection of village, there is a nice park with shops and bars on the perimeter. I stopped for awhile and watched people order and eat at the largest bar with tables outside and decided that it looked expensive and not what I wanted just then. What I did want was a decent and inexpensive sit-down lunch in a nice restaurant. I crossed the street and walked north a few steps to where there were several restaurants to choose from, so I selected one and found that it was just what I wanted. Nicely decorated with several square tables in a medium size room overlooking a small courtyard. Mama in the kitchen and her daughter was the waitress. I ordered a roast pork dinner with soup, salad, and tortilla. The meal was perfect except for the coffee. Apparently only the bars have the coffee makers that produce one cup at a time of excellent coffee. I gathered myself together and headed out. A few hundred meters out of village, just before el Camino turned off the paved road, I passed a resort where the horses were resting on the front lawn. From here it was 15.3 km to Santa Irene, my destination for the day. That would make a total of 26.5 km from Melide where I started this morning. Not too bad for a cripple. The walk to Santa Irene was relatively pleasant considering my hip problem, which acted up occasionally, and at about 7:00 I crested the hill on the highway just before Santa Irene which has two restaurants, one on each side of the road, and walked down the hill to the Refugio. The place was brimming with pilgrims, mostly Spanish students, and as I checked in I must have been visibly concerned about being thrown into the large dorm with them. After registering with the woman in charge and getting my credentials stamped she directed me to a room at the front of the first floor. The room had only two double bunk beds, which were occupied, except for one bed. I was quite relieved and she could see my gratitude. It was almost as though she was holding the bed especially for me. It's not that I had a problem with bunking in with crowds, since I have done my share, but I was particularly tired this day and the group at the Refugio was particularly raucous. Two Dutch girls occupied one of the bunk beds and Cas, a middle aged man from Holland occupied the other. Of course they were getting along famously, and I seemed to fit in reasonably well. They were kind enough to speak English once I arrived, giving up their native tongue. We talked about language for a minute, and how unique theirs is, and unique sounding. I asked them to carry on in Dutch for awhile just to let the flavor of the language sink in. It is one of the oddest sounding languages I've heard, with much guttural rumbling and tongue clucking. I enjoyed their company enormously. After unpacking, I went outside to consider my dinner options and was joined by Cas. We decided to dine together at one of the restaurants at the top of the hill and started walking the kilometer back to them. When we reached the top of the hill, we were faced with a choice and went for the restaurant on the right. Once inside, we were informed that the place was closed, so we crossed the highway to the other one, which was very nice, spacious and comfortable feeling. We sat at a table and talked as we waited for our food to arrive. It turns out that Cas, like just about every other Hollander I have met, is a councilor. He was making the pilgrimage because he was about to change professions from councilor to minister in the community he lives. He was in transition.

This led us to a discussion of the various reasons people make this pilgrimage and we came up with the following list:

1. Life transition.
2. Cultural tourist.
3. Architectural tourist.
4. Sport. Many young people do it just for the physical challenge.
5. Religious. Faith and the desire for atonement have motivated pilgrims for centuries.
6. Healing. This is the "less than a full shilling" category, broadly defining people who are suffering.
7. Spiritual.
8. Bereavement.

We enjoyed our conversation, and after finishing our dinner we headed back to the Refugio. Once there we found the girls had already turned in and we did the same, anticipating tomorrow's 19.5 km walk to our final destination: Santiago de Compostela.

New suburban dwelling.

July 24
Santa Irene–Santiago de Compostela

When I awoke to the crowds of students preparing to depart, I gathered my gear together and went outside to assess the morning. Since I remembered to take an ibuprofen pill last night the hip pain was under control, unlike yesterday when I could hardly stand when I awoke. Dozens of kids were playing around in front of the Refugio, some talking some packing their things, but all seemed to be in very high spirits. I sat on a bench at the front of the building lacing up my boots and arranging my pack. Suddenly we were all splashed with a torrent of water as one of the young bucks sprayed the crowd from a water bottle. Everyone within range scattered, myself included. Much hearty shouting and laughing followed. Ah, the energy of youthful hormones. The first to depart were the Dutch girls, who, when they got across the road, were uncertain of the correct direction. From our side of the road the question was intensely debated and directions shouted to them. The final decision was to continue on the road and not go across the field as they originally intended. Leaving Santa Irene. The walk from Santa Irene is partly on the road followed by a path through forest paths eventually opening up to a broad field peppered with houses under construction. The construction techniques here in Spain are completely different from those in the U.S. where we still build private homes mostly from wood. Here, the chief building material is concrete, and as I walked through the field I passed one house after another being built from this material. The frame is entirely concrete: foundation, walls, and upper floors. I thought it curious the way the second story concrete forms were supported by what seemed to be a random forest of temporary columns holding it up as the concrete cured.

Leaving Santa Irene.

When a giant passenger jet roared into view as it approached Lavacolla Airport, I knew that my pilgrimage was truly coming to an end. I stopped for a beer in a bar in San Paio before embarking on the final trek upwards to

Monte del Gozo. I decided to pass on stripping down naked and bathing in the Lavacolla River even though it is a long-standing tradition. I reasoned that since I had actually been bathing regularly, my body odor probably wasn't bad enough to offend the Apostle, unlike the pilgrims of medieval times. The flavor of el Camino had definitely taken on a distinctly urban air. Many more people were in the villages and they were neither pilgrims nor natives. Each step brought me closer to the dense civilization I started from, a fact that I both regretted and looked forward to. Traversing the top of Monte del Gozo along the paved road was somewhat less than a spectacular finale to a pilgrimage that had wound its way through some of the finest countryside available anywhere. Yet, here I was watching the T.V. station towers draw nearer as I walked through the low bushes fringing the road. After what seemed longer than it actually was due to my anticipation, I arrived at the summit. Here I found crowds of people, mostly bussed in, milling around the small compound and photographing each other in front of the hideous monument on the lawn. I walked over to it but, sadly, I couldn't actually pick out the spires of the cathedral that were supposedly visible from the spot. Seriously anticlimactic to be sure. Disappointed, I proceeded down the hill past the gigantic hostel complex where I was planning to check in until I saw it. For all the world, it looked exactly like a military barracks, and I simply could not bring myself to enter. I knew that this was the eve of the festival in Santiago de Compostela and that there would likely not be a single bed to be had in village. Still I decided to pass on the hostel. In addition to its uninviting appearance, this Refugio was far from the old city where the cathedral was located and where I planned to spend my time. Even further than I thought, it turned out. At the foot of the hill, I crossed a footbridge over the eight-lane highway and proceeded on a sidewalk through the city.

Plaza de las Platerias.

At some point I must have lost my way, though I doubt if it delayed my arrival by much since I was heading in the right direction. I stopped in a small store and bought a soft drink and got directions from the owner. I literally walked for hours before I arrived at the Cathedral at the Plaza de la Platerias. The light was beautiful and a man was playing bagpipes, especially to celebrate my arrival I assumed, and it was wonderful. I had been on the road for 37 days and arrived at exactly the right moment to participate in the gala celebration that was to begin at midnight and that had brought people to Santiago from all over Europe. The air was electrified with anticipation, and clearly, people were already deep into celebrating. In my own understated way I was elated. The tradition for pilgrims arriving at the Cathedral is to approach the magnificent Portico de la Gloria and place his hands on the Tree of Jesse on the central column, above which sits St. James himself. Knowing this, I dutifully headed for the Portico and found the spot at the base of the column, the marble of which was deeply worn by millions of pilgrims over the centuries. I knelt down and placed my fingers on the column saying a silent prayer of thanks to St. James for bringing my pilgrimage safely to a conclusion. Then, also according to tradition, I knelt again and touched foreheads with a likeness Master Mateo, the architect responsible for this masterpiece. The cathedral was crowded with tourists and T.V. crews were setting up near the alter to document the Mass tomorrow. I left in search of the registrar to present my credentials and receive my official certificate of completing the pilgrimage.

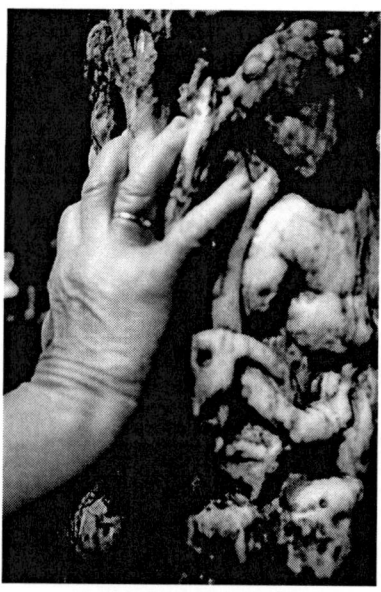

Pilgrim's hand on the Tree of Jesse.

The gift shop sent me across the plaza where, on route, I was further directed by a man who recognized how lost I was. When I arrived at Number 1 Rua del Villar, only a few feet off the plaza, I went to the second floor and found a calamitous scene. There was a queue stretching from the room down the hall and pilgrims were crowded into the room like sardines in a can. Inside, the scribes were preparing the certificates with the recipients name written in Latin, an ongoing tradition from the 14th century. To make matters more interesting, there was a Japanese video crew taping the proceedings for Tokyo television. The event was quite fun really, and I met several people whom I had encountered at one time or another along the way. When it was my turn I presented my credential (the passport that each Refugio stamped along the way) to the official who asked my name and proceeded to fill out the pre-printed certificate.

Pilgrims being taped as they receive their certificate.

All the while the video crew taped, and I presume the brief transaction would be used to amuse a Japanese housewife some afternoon. On my way out I spoke with Nick briefly who was staying at the barrack Refugio back at Monte del Gozo. He told me that the place was mobbed and that they had him sleeping on the floor, a detail confirming my intuitive decision to pass on the place. Now I needed to find a place to sleep for the night, and while this was somewhat urgent, I didn't feel particularly panicked by the situation. I suppose I had become accustomed to not knowing where I would sleep until the last minute. I left the building and walked up the hill along one of the quaint cobbled streets of the old city. I had no idea where I was going, but upon cresting the summit and continuing a few doors, I stopped at a café and sat at a very pleasant table on the street to rest and have a café solo.

The Certificate.

When I asked the waitress/owner in my practically non-existent Spanish if she knew of any place for a poor pilgrim to sleep, she told me that she had a friend who ran a hotel around the corner who might have something. She immediately went off to collect her friend and returned with her after a few minutes. When the discussion began with how crowded the city was and how scarce rooms were, I knew I was in for a very high price. As expected, she quoted a very dear price for a room for three days, and I politely told her

Table at the cafe where I found a room.

that I would consider it and get back to her. After she left, my hostess confided in me that she had a room available—her eldest son's room who was away at the time. I was, of course elated, and jumped at the invitation to see it. On the way upstairs past the bar she drove home the conditions that were mainly that I don't disturb anything, since all of her son's possessions were still in the room exactly as he had left them. Of course I solemnly agreed not to touch anything and she quoted me a very attractive price of 2400 Pts. for the three —paid in advance. This was less than her friend's price for a single night and I instantly accepted it. Once again St. James had come through to help a pitiful pilgrim! I thanked him silently and settled in for a shower and nap before the evening's festivities.

Around 9:00 P.M. I awoke and went downstairs for a café con lèche and something to eat. The woman's husband took care of the bar and they had delightful son who was about 8 years old. Now that I was an official guest, I was treated with great warmth and hospitality. They were a charming and gracious couple that went out of their way to make me feel comfortable. After eating I headed down to the cathedral to check out the activities. The streets were crowded with people and everyone was in a party mood. Boisterous groups of young men sang and drank as they roamed through the streets and plazas surrounding the cathedral. It was a gigantic celebration and I felt jubilant just being there as a witness. Later, as midnight approached, the crowds were growing, and I thought I would go down into the Plaza del Obradoiro, the large main plaza in front of the cathedral. I followed the flow of people in that direction and when I reached the entrance to the plaza the scene was incredible. Music was playing and people were packed in so tight that I had no idea how more were being accommodated. I knew that there were fireworks arranged in front of the cathedral and that people were crowding in to witness them. I couldn't handle it, and like the similar scene in Burgos, I fought my way back out against the tide of people almost immediately. Once free I felt greatly relieved and retreated to the Plaza de las Platerías—my favorite plaza of those that surround the cathedral.

Detail of the Cathedral.

It is small with a beautiful fountain and a wide staircase up to the cathedral doors graced with elegantly carved columns on either side. Here there were relatively few people and I found a seat and watched in awe as the fireworks display commenced. While the fireworks were designed to be seen from the Plaza del Obradoiro, they were nonetheless amazing from my vantage point. They seemed to be set off from the roof of the cathedral itself and I was so close that I could hear the whoosh and roar of the rockets as they shot up into the sky. The sound, in fact, was deafening, and the spectacle was awe inspiring as the fireworks exploded directly overhead. I have no idea how they avoided having the entire city burn to a cinder given the enormous quantity of sparks and explosives that were let loose into the sky above it.

Detail of the Cathedral.

I sat amazed and convinced that the celebration was arranged on my behalf to commemorate my completing the pilgrimage. This really was a perfect way to celebrate the completion of the most difficult and challenging undertaking of my life to date and I felt elated and privileged to participate. When the fireworks ended people began to disperse and I sat wondering where I would find some food since I hadn't eaten supper yet. I decided to head in the general direction of the crowds, which was straight to the area where nightclubs, bars, and restaurants were located. The streets were packed wall-to-wall with people carousing and having a good time. I walked around for awhile and after passing a brightly lit bar I stopped for some reason and turned around and went back. Something told me to go in, which I did, and I stood at the bar and ordered a beer. In a few minutes Win, a woman I had encountered many times throughout el Camino, came through the door with several of her friends and we greeted each other warmly. Then I noticed that Evelyn was sitting at a table with her friend Jean-Batiste, and she came over and invited me to join them for dinner. Evelyn is from France and a journalist writing a story on el Camino. We enjoyed a wonderful dinner in the crowded bar over conversation about our various adventures. Of the hundreds of bars in Santiago de Compostela it was really quite magical that we should converge on this particular one on this night. At about 3:30 A.M. we finished, said our good-byes and departed. I walked into a small plaza were a rock band was playing and realized that I had no idea whatsoever where my hostel was located. Then, to complete the magic of the evening,

I followed my feet a few dozen meters and found my hostel waiting for me right where I left it.

Inside the Cathedral.

July 25

Mass in the Cathedral.

My pilgrimage was officially over. I went to Mass at the cathedral, which was attended by thousands. The priests lit the giant silver botafumeiro and swung it back and forth over the crowds to their delight while the state T.V. documented the entire event. I spent the day resting and photographing around the cathedral and will take a train to Madrid tomorrow to catch a flight back to the U.S. It was done and finished and I had survived. More than that, I had learned a great deal about what I was capable of, about not giving up, and about Grace—especially about Grace, since I certainly couldn't have completed the pilgrimage without it. As I write this journal two and a half years later I am still learning from the experience. In fact, the importance I place on it is only now becoming clear to me. This pilgrimage, like any, is on one level a metaphor for the journey we all take through life and its secrets will continue to unfold as long as the Way of St. James holds a place in my heart.

fin

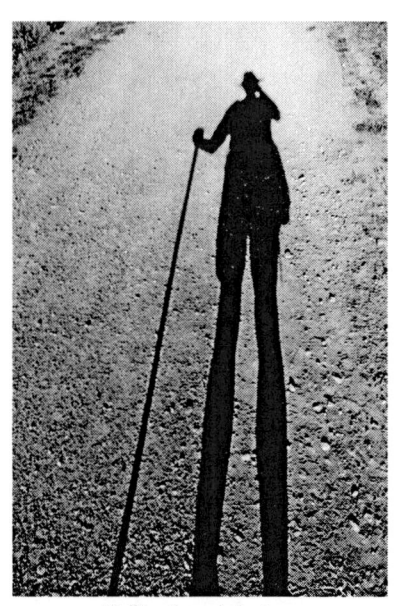

Walking through shadows.

Resources

A Practical Guide for Pilgrims, Editorial Everest; ISBN: 84-241-3833-3

© 2011 Carl Sesto

www.sabbaticalpress.com